# THE STRANGERS

# THE STRANGERS

## Matthew Manning

First published in 1978
First paperback edition published in 1995 by Colin Smythe Limited,
Gerrards Cross, Buckinghamshire SL9 8XA

ISBN 0-86140-387-8

*Acknowledgements*
I should like to thank John Childerley for his painstaking work on the
plan of Queen's House, John Redman for most of the photographs, and
the Cambridge City Library for permission to reproduce the photographs
of nineteenth century Linton.

Printed in Great Britain
Printed and bound by The Guernsey Press Company Ltd.,
Vale, Guernsey, C.I.

For 'Robert Webbe'
(1664–1703 and 1686–1736)
whose presence having
been revealed, advanced
to other levels of
existence.

Time present and time past
Are both perhaps present in time future,
And time future contained in time past.
If all time is eternally present
All time is unredeemable.
What might have been is an abstraction
Remaining a perpetual possibility
Only in a world of speculation.
What might have been and what has been
Point to one end, which is always present.


From 'Burnt Norton',
    by T. S. Eliot.

# Contents

# *Illustrations*

# Introduction

From the time I first conceived the idea of writing a book about Robert Webbe I was aware that it would be very much like breaking open a hornets' nest. It seemed to me that I could easily get stung because of the nature of the contents of the book. I decided that one way of preventing myself from being hurt too badly was by careful timing.

Perhaps at this early stage I should explain a little about my abilities and my experiences for the benefit of people who may not have read about me elsewhere.

In 1974 I wrote a book entitled *The Link* which described how, at the age of eleven, the home in which I lived with my parents and younger brother and sister became the scene of strange manifestations which we realised were produced by a poltergeist. It was I, rather than my brother or sister, who was thought, by Professor George Owen who investigated the case to be the source of the disturbances. My parents were assured that in a few weeks the phenomena would cease and our family could settle down to live normally again. As predicted, the poltergeist's activities diminished after about three months. However, when I was fifteen the phenomena recurred with far greater power and violence. By now I was a boarder at a public school. Chaos ensued as parents worried about pupils at the school, or that I might be contagious. At one stage I was even asked to carry out rituals of exorcism in the hope that it would quell the poltergeist phenomena. It was by accident that I stumbled across a solution which stopped the destructive force of the poltergeist. By allowing myself to be used by some unknown force or forces, the hitherto destructive powers now created the most beautiful drawings, and wrote extraordinary scripts signed by people whom we knew had died. One of these was a gentleman who signed himself, 'Rob: Webbe'.

Later on I discovered that I could affect electrical circuits, amongst other things, in a strange way. Clocks would stop, light bulbs would illuminate, and if I appeared on radio or TV the sound system would become broken or distorted.

For nearly two years I placed myself at the disposal of various scientists all over the world so that I could be tested under controlled conditions. Initially I enjoyed participating in these experiments and I believe that my co-operation benefited both the researchers and myself. Within a very short period of time some remarkable discoveries were made and, in Canada, a brain-wave pattern unlike anything previously recorded was observed. However, all these experiments have been reported and detailed elsewhere, in official reports and in my second book published in 1977, entitled, *In the Minds of Millions*.

Gradually I became less enthusiastic about these experiments, and more disillusioned—even cynical—about the so-called science of parapsychology. I was constantly made to repeat the same experiments, not because the scientists did not believe me, but because they did not believe the findings of their fellow scientists.

I was also beginning to realize that most of the experiments in which I was being engaged involved the destruction or disruption of physical systems. Nobody was interested in devising experiments concerned with my mental abilities, which produced phenomena like automatic writing and drawing and telepathy, as opposed to influencing compass needles, or lighting electric bulbs.

Certainly physical phenomena were of great interest, but I was becoming dissatisfied. I shall not delve further into that growing disenchantment other than to say that in March, 1976, I decided that I was going to withdraw for a couple of years from participating in controlled experiments of a physical nature. I have described how I came to this decision in my book, *In the Minds of Millions*.

During those months of experiments, many of them conducted by the world's leading scientists, I noticed a very marked abhorrence on the part of the scientists to the idea of a life after death. Many of them seemed terrified of such ideas, and for that reason were loath to consider experiments involving my automatic writing or drawing. There were, of course, exceptions, but even they would not admit publicly to a belief in life after death. Professor Hans Bender, the leading European parapsychologist from Freiburg University in Germany, once told me that he believed in life after death, but it was not worth risking his reputation to state this belief publicly. And so he remains, in the eyes of the public, as a man who holds animistic theories about alleged communications with the dead. It is all explicable in terms of telepathy, or the ludicrous 'Super-ESP', as far as he is concerned publicly. Privately, his views are different.

All the time I had engaged in these experiments, I had the outline of this book in my mind, and I felt a growing compulsion to record all the events with which it deals, partly as an act of defiance against the myopia of the scientists. I wanted to be able to write this book and be in a position where it really did not matter to me what anybody else thought. It is a true story and one which I hope will be worthy of the reader's belief.

I was also struck by the fact that, in general, the press was (or journalists were) only prepared to write about me because I had a 'certificate of approval' from the scientists. If I had not had their backing, I would not have been taken seriously. The strange fact was that my story was the same, regardless of whether it was corroborated by scientists or not.

Therefore I decided to challenge both the scientists and the press with my own one-man rebellion. I have no doubt that I shall be heavily criticised over the contents of this book. My critics will call it unscientific. But I am no longer concerned about this. *The Strangers* is not intended to be a scientific work. It deals with the spiritual side of the psychic world in which I found myself, as opposed to the physical side, with which the scientific experiments were concerned. If you want to read about the amazement of scientists when I destroy an electrical circuit, you will not find it in these pages. The spiritual aspect of the psychic world is as important as the physical aspect, if not more so, because the spiritual ultimately affects each of us. Nobody escapes from it. It seemed to me that this was the principal reason for scientists' fear of the spiritual aspects of the psyche.

Physical phenomena can be viewed objectively, at a safe distance, and need not affect the viewers, but the spiritual is too personal. If scientists were to investigate the spiritual they would lose their objectivity because as it involved them, it would become a subjective experience. The result would be that they would end up taking themselves apart to discover a little more of how they ticked. Also the physical can be measured with electrodes, feeding data to graphs; spiritual things cannot be mathematically measured and recorded.

It was therefore with the intention of writing this book, and of pursuing the spiritual aspects of my abilities, that I disengaged myself for a while from controlled experiments. I felt that my abilities were on two different levels, but that I had been concentrating on one at the expense of the other. Everything had, I felt, become unbalanced and in need of adjustment.

I must state at this stage that my interest in the former occupants of my home, Queen's House, had been sparked off some time before Robert Webbe made himself known. On a red brick set into an outside wall of the house is scratched, 'J. Webb 1731', and it was this which had inspired me to try to discover more about the history of the house and the village in which it stood.

I therefore spent two mornings in 1970 searching the original Linton Parish Registers for clues about former occupants of the house. (When I returned seven years later to research the many facts that Robert Webbe had supplied in his automatic writing, I found it much easier to study these registers, as they had been transcribed and type-written; previously they were still in the original handwriting, dating back to the late sixteenth century, which is not easy to read, especially for somebody who is aged fifteen.) During that first visit, of course, it is likely that I saw some of the names which subsequently appeared on the walls of the house. However, digging into the history of Linton is an arduous task, as any researcher will soon discover, because the village is built along the banks of the River Granta which used frequently to burst its banks before it was dredged and deepened after serious flooding of the village in 1968; this has resulted in many documents being destroyed by floodwater and other hazards of time. This is especially true of the Parish Registers which were kept in the church, close to the river, until after the 1968 floods.

In fact the only place where the Parish Registers might have had any significant bearing upon the Webbe phenomena is in the case of the signatures which appeared on the wall. Little of the information subsequently provided by Robert Webbe could have been gleaned from this source. (Even if one were to dismiss the writing on the wall and the automatic writing, both of which have in any case been amply witnessed by others, there are still a large number of other phenomena remaining.) Other evidence such as the smell of tobacco smoke have to be accounted for too.

I believe that seeing the Linton Parish Registers was the catalyst that precipitated the eruption of strange occurrences associated with Robert Webbe. I also suspect that the same sort of thing would have occurred in whatever house I happened to live—and, for all I know, it may happen again in a different building. It is for the reader to judge what part my viewing of the Parish Registers played in the appearance of the ensuing phenomena, and probably there will be differences of opinion about this.

I have no doubt that many of the scientists with whom I have collaborated will be somewhat shocked that I should have decided to write what they will consider an 'unscientific' story. But for me, the events described in this book are real, just as real as those events witnessed, and often recorded, when I have been involved in experiments with scientists. If they do choose to believe my story, they will devise all sorts of intricate theories about how these things could have happened, in a desperate attempt to deny that it is in any way connected with the enigma

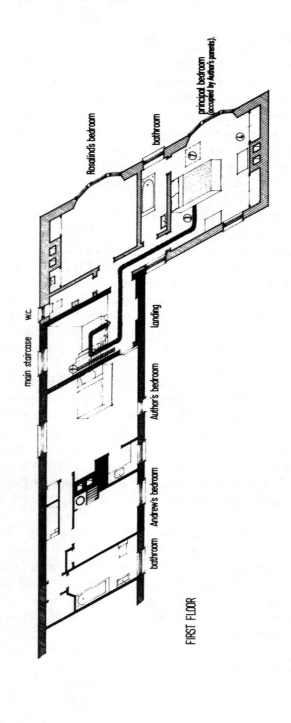

main staircase    w.c.

Rosalind's bedroom

bathroom

principal bedroom
(occupied by Author's parents).

landing

Author's bedroom

Andrew's bedroom

bathroom

FIRST FLOOR

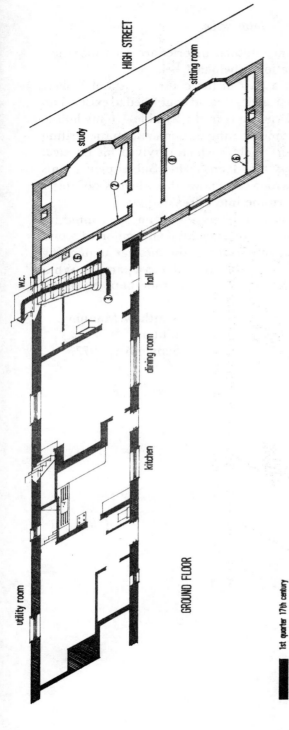

HIGH STREET

study

sitting room

w.c.

hall

dining room

kitchen

utility room

GROUND FLOOR

▮ 1st quarter 17th century
▮ 3rd quarter 17th century
▨ 1731

① Route taken by Robert Webbe, from the quarter landing to the top of the staircase.

② Indication of the walls with the signatures inscribed upon them.

③ Route along which apports were discovered - from the bed in the principal bedroom to the bottom of the main staircase.

④ Position at which Webbe stood in the principal bedroom on our second meeting.

⑤ The room in which the lighted candle was found placed upon the floor.

⑥ The glass-fronted cabinet from which the tokens were removed.

⑦ The cupboard/hole in the floor of the principal bedroom in which the 'lost' framed prints were found.

⑧ Picture.

of life after death. To me, all their theories are even more unlikely than the explanation in which I believe.

I hold the view that a part of the consciousness of Robert Webbe survived his physical death, and continued to exist—I do not say 'live', because I cannot regard it as a life—in my house. I believe that I was communicating through automatic writing with that part of Robert Webbe which survived his physical death. But who is to say that I am right? Subsequent events may prove my views wrong. Anyhow, these beliefs do not, I hope, automatically turn me into a freak.

I hope that this book will be read with an open mind, as it probably would be if it were a scientifically endorsed work. The contents are not as important as the message underlying the story. Even if it *is* unbelievable, regard it as a parable. What happened to Robert Webbe could some time happen also to YOU.

Matthew Manning,
Linton.
September, 1977.

# One:     *'My visit will be long or short, just as you please.'*

The room was very nearly dark except for a frail beam of light which fell through the gap in the curtains from the street light outside.

In a short while, the room became quite dark, as the light outside was switched off. The church clock chimed a solemn twelve strokes away in the distant night and my father knew that it was now past midnight.

He drifted back and forth through soft, nebulous barriers of light sleep until time became irrelevant.

He could not remember how much later it was when he found himself in the mouth of a large cave, looking out at a kaleidoscope sky of varying hues of violet and purple. The colours were ebbing and flowing, pulsating, sometimes brighter around the edges and then brighter in the centre.

Where the cave was, or how he came to be in it, he could not recall; he was quietly content to lie watching the beautiful sky above him. The alternating intensities of the violet shades reminded him of clouds passing over the sun on a fine day.

Gradually he became aware that his eyes were closed despite the apparently vivid reality of the scene in which he found himself. It seemed too real to be merely the result of imagination but his sense of rationality told him that there could not possibly be a sun in the sky because it was night time. Neither had he gone to bed in a cave as far as he could remember.

The scene continued to persist although it had been attacked with rational thinking. The sky remained swirling around the mouth of the cave in whose entrance he still lay. He could even see boulders littered around the opening of the cave, silhouetted against the sky like teeth.

Teeth—an analogy suddenly struck him.

With some dismay he became aware that his own eyes were in the centre of somebody else's open mouth and he was looking out through their teeth. What he had at first mistaken for boulders were teeth.

Next he heard a scratching sound as of a man's stubbled chin rubbing against the sheets next to his left cheek. It was a sound which he had heard on several occasions before this particular night; it was not his own chin because the noise continued even when he lay quite motionless.

Robert Webbe was in bed too.

Although still impressed by the beautiful hues of violet and purple, he willed that these colours should change to shades of green. Nothing happened.

Instead he now felt his body being alternately compressed and stretched, as if he was fixed to a rack. At the same time he felt what he thought was a large hand being rubbed up and down over his body. It was quite heavy rubbing, almost as if somebody was trying to massage his body from the other side of the bedclothes. It was not uncomfortable but almost soothing in a strange way; although he was by now fully awake and alert he could not bring himself to make the effort to try and grab this hand. He was quite content to remain in this pleasurable state.

The colours were now beginning to intensify as if in defiance of the fact that my father had willed that they should change. As this occurred the lower half of his right leg began to tingle, as it had done on previous occasions.

Now, for the first time since this strange experience had swept over him, he gingerly opened one eye, half hoping that he was hallucinating and that it was all imagined.

With one eye open, and then the other, he was still able to see the brilliant shades of violet, but only in the lower half of his field of vision. With the opening of his eyes the tingling sensation spread from the lower half of his right leg to the entire lower half of his body.

'Go away. I have had enough. I must have sleep,' chided my father in his mind.

He repeated this several times and slowly felt a certain sense of upheaval as though a 'departure' was actually occurring. He continued the mental instructions in a more agressive, bullying fashion and was surprised at the apparent connection between his instructions and the tingling sensations.

Silently he told Webbe,

'Go away. I shall tell Matthew.'

This he repeated several times and again there was a widespread tingling. After a short while he repeated my name four times with no other words at all.

'Matthew, Matthew, Matthew, Matthew.'

The tingling sensations flared up at each mention of my name. He again opened his eyes and was now able to see not only the characteristic purple colour but also a topaz yellow colour, although both were waning rapidly.

Soon both colours had drained away into the darkness of the night and Robert Webbe left the bed.

It was December 17th, 1974. It was because all this happened then, that nobody was very surprised at my father's experiences when he related them the next morning. After all, it was Christmas time and after six years in Queen's House we knew that we could expect strange phenomena at this time of the year (as well as in mid-summer). We had all become accustomed to these odd happenings which occurred without warning in certain areas of the house. We were not frightened or worried— why should we have been? Robert Webbe had become almost a friend; much more than a shadow.

Robert Webbe had introduced himself about three years after we moved into the house, in 1968. I remember the first incident quite clearly—it is not the kind of thing that one quickly forgets. I was sixteen years old when the episode I am about to describe occurred.

It was a dark cold November evening and I was at home with my sister, Rosalind, who was thirteen at the time. She was upstairs in her bedroom while I was downstairs in a room which at that time was my bedroom.

As my parents had briefly gone into the village, I was not

really surprised when I heard a rapping on my door. My parents had obviously returned home so I got up and opened the door. Nobody was there.

My first thought was that my sister was playing a joke to frighten me so I closed the door again. At this moment I wasn't frightened because I really thought that Rosalind was knocking on the door. A few minutes later there were another three raps on the door. I leapt to my feet, flung open the door and, seeing that my sister had apparently run away, I chased upstairs to her bedroom.

She was asleep in bed and it was quite clear that she had not left her room at any time during the previous five minutes.

Now I was worried. I knew that I was unable to explain the knocking on the door, unless of course I had been imagining it. But I was sure that it really had occurred. I returned somewhat warily to my room, shutting the door behind me. This time I sat near to the door so that I could open it as soon as the rapping occurred again—if it were to do so.

Within two minutes or so, three sharp, clear raps came from the other side of the door. I opened it immediately and again there was nobody to be seen. The house was absolutely silent—nobody was running away. I felt my heart beating more heavily.

But the house was not to remain silent. Another tapping noise came from the top of the staircase. I was unable to see this part of the staircase from my position in the hall so I walked over to the foot of the stairs and looked up.

There at the top of the stairs was a burglar looking straight down at me. I stood immobilized with fear and surprise, and an uneasy feeling of helplessness. What should I do? How had he got into the house? Should I run? A thousand confused thoughts raced through my mind in those few seconds. He seemed as frightened of me as I was of him. Instead of using threatening behaviour as I expected him to, he just stood where he was. Although he was not moving, I noticed that he was swaying slightly as he tried to support himself on a pair of sticks.

What was a burglar doing with a pair of sticks? He could

not be a very effective criminal if he was dependent upon such supports. Then it suddenly hit me, as I noticed his very odd clothes—this was no burglar. It must be an apparition.

And yet he appeared quite solid—in fact solid enough for me to have mistaken him for a real human being, had his clothes not given him away. I saw that he wore a green coloured frock coat which was embroidered around the edges with a yellow thread; it displayed large buttons down the front, and large cuffs which were also embroidered. It seemed to have no collar, although this section of the garment was partially covered by a large brown wig which fell in ringlets over his stocky shoulders. Frilled cuffs flowed out from around his wrists, showing that he was wearing a creamy coloured shirt. Tied around his neck was a long cream cravat made of what looked to me like lace.

Between his frock coat and the shirt was a rather plain and simple waistcoat, buttoned from top to bottom and displaying a pocket on each side at about waist-level. He wore breeches which reached down to his knees; below that he wore cream coloured stockings which appeared to be knitted. All the while I stared at him he supported himself rather uneasily on a pair of rough sticks. His feet were obscured by the side of the staircase because of my angle of view.

While I stood dumbfounded, he spoke in a perfectly ordinary human voice, without any trace of an accent. It sounded like the voice of a man tired after making an effort to walk with difficulty, almost as if he was out of breath.

'I must offer you my most humble apology for giving you so much fright, but I must walk for my blessed legs,' he said, apparently aware that he had frightened me.

For what seemed like minutes, although retrospectively I doubt if it was more than fifteen seconds, I said nothing. I just stood, heart pounding, watching him descend with some difficulty seven stairs until he reached the second turn on the staircase. I remember being surprised that he was having such difficulty in walking—I imagined that ghosts floated with ease.

I didn't know what to do, although by now my sense of initiative was returning. Several things occurred to me in quick succession. I thought of trying to photograph him but I realized that the only camera in the house was a rather old model belonging to my father. In any case, it would be quite useless, I thought, as it had no flash light attachment and the light was not good enough to take a photograph without one. (Later I discovered that the camera had no film in it anyway.)

Strangely enough, it never occurred to me to ask him who he was in my fearfulness. Instead I said to him,

'Would you mind staying here please, while I fetch something.'

I was conscious of trying to be polite to him, more because I was frightened of him than out of any desire to make him stay. I automatically assumed that he could see me, hear me, and understand me, and it was not until later that it struck me as odd that he complied with my request.

I rushed to the kitchen, grabbed an old used envelope and a pencil and returned to the stairs. He was still there, though he had descended another three stairs.

I could now see that he was wearing high-heeled shoes which looked worn and unpolished; they displayed large tongues reaching up and covering his insteps. Adorning the front of each shoe was a single plain silver buckle. I also noticed that his two sticks had no ferrules on their ends.

I stood on the bottom flight of stairs and made a shaky sketch of him. It was while drawing him that I noticed a very strong spicy smell. All the while I was worried that he would vanish or fade away before my sketch was completed.

To my surprise, I heard him mutter something about it being cold, which it certainly was not as the central heating we had installed was full on. He turned on his heels and walked up the stairs much more quickly and with greater ease, apparently, than he had when he descended them. I remember thinking that he had got up the stairs far faster than I would have expected of someone supported by a pair of sticks.

He apparently disappeared somewhere between the landing

and my parents' bedroom and the house was restored to quiet normality.

It did not really seem that normality had been much disturbed. I started to think about what had happened. Had I perhaps imagined it all? If I had imagined it though, I reasoned with myself, why was I holding this sketch of a man wearing old-fashioned clothes?

I told my parents this strange tale when they arrived home shortly afterwards; although interested, they were not as surprised as I expected they might be. Maybe the poltergeist events of preceding times, which I have described in my book, *The Link*, had persuaded them that nothing was really impossible where I was concerned.

Some months after this experience I found in the bottom of a cupboard, a project that I had written for a history examination at school. I found in it something that I had written which I had completely forgotten and which convinced me that what I had seen on the staircase was not the result of an over-fervent imagination.

I had to write a project for part of an 'O-level' examination at school for history. I chose to write about the history of Linton, since I had already tried, unsuccessfully, to trace the previous owners of the house through the Linton Parish Registers. As I have stated, I was unable to find very much information, due partly to the fact that probably many documents which might have been of assistance to me were locked away in libraries and records offices, etc., to which school boys could not easily gain access.

In my project, however, I had described what I imagined an eighteenth-century country gentleman would wear.

'He would probably wear the fashionable wide skirted coat of red with deep flap pockets ... the shirt would have been frilled and a black Steenkirk cravat would be worn around the neck. A short black periwig in bobs gathered into bunches on the shoulders and twisted in a small bob at the back of the neck would have been worn ...'

I think that if I had experienced an hallucination on the

staircase, I would have seen a man wearing these clothes, and not the ones which I did see. There are a number of differences between what I would have expected to see, and what I saw. The man on the stairs was not wearing a red coat, and it was not particularly widely skirted; his cravat was black, not cream. The most noticeable difference was in the wigs; I saw a person wearing a long flowing wig, although in my mind I had previously imagined that he would wear a short black wig, gathered at the back almost in a ponytail fashion.

I do not doubt that there *was* a connection between the apparition I saw and this school project of mine. Indeed, Robert Webbe later claimed that it was because I was missing so much information from my project that he decided to help me by producing 'halfe a thousande' names that would be of assistance to me. That had been the beginning and since that time we had lived with a shadow lodger in our house.

But was it our house? The question of ownership, as we were to discover, was one of the reasons why Robert Webbe was still with us although he had apparently died in 1733.

One morning in June 1971 I had been writing automatically at home, more to prevent another outbreak of poltergeist activity than for any other reason, when I produced a message in strange sprawling handwriting and odd spelling.

'Your worke on our familye was most goode and very righte. I have sene you at the top of myne stairs very maney times. Do not take offence I must wander for the malades and wretched sores upon my very legs. I will see you tonight nowe. Your sister must see me in my room. I mean the room that is placed next my closet cupboard. Do not worry about the noyse. I am so used to blessed mad horse. I am very proude of my house so I walke in it often. Soon I will appear to you all. Some days my legs are so mightey painfull indeede I can scarce warlke to my roome. So I trip and clutch the windows. I do offere my humbel apologies if I disturbe any of you. Tonite. You can do nowt for my legges. Indeed I feare they may soon be severred from my very bodey or else I shall die. Try and comfort my poore wife Mary who weeps every morning in my bedchamber as my legs rotte before oure eyes. She knows I will surely die. And sits on your bedde which is too soft for my leggs. I stand at the top of my stairs when the houre of my departure is nigh. My son is ... ', and he trailed off, signing himself as Robert Webbe and placing a date, 1733, under his signature.

My parents and I wondered if this communication was maybe connected to two strange incidents which had occurred just a few weeks earlier. The first had happened at about seven o'clock one Sunday morning when my brother, Andrew, who was aged eleven, had got up early and had gone to wake up my sister.

As they sat on her bed talking quietly, both heard somebody walking down the uncarpeted stairs, although they knew that nobody else had yet risen. It struck them as odd immediately they heard the noise as they realized that they had not heard anybody walk down the landing in order to reach the staircase. The sound appeared to them like someone walking in wooden clogs. Curiosity overcame their initial fright and they crept out of the bedroom to peer over the banisters at the top of the staircase.

Nobody was there and as soon as they looked over the banisters the noise abruptly ceased.

The second incident occurred at about the same time. I had come home late one night when everybody else was already in bed and the house was in darkness except for a small amount of light which slipped through the windows from a half-moon. As I stood in the hallway I distinctly heard somebody walk along the uncarpeted landing directly above me. I assumed that it was either my mother or father checking that I had arrived home safely, so I walked to the bottom of the stairs and turned round to wish them goodnight.

At the top of the stairs I saw the figure of a man and in the gloom, I assumed it was my father. I told him I was home and was a little surprised that, as he had bothered to get out of bed, he did not answer me.

I said goodnight to him and retired to bed. The following

7.1.72

Did you light our candles?
Why I must admit to having being
done. I should envy my gratitude for you
giving to me in the rooms they like fine candles
which are to much better than those that
I have. They candles make so little money.
Why did you place one candle in the water-closet.
I know not the water closet yourself my
if but I did place one of my candles in
my lavatory which way looking on ge fame.
How do you light the candles?
Why I done how I always like my candles
And how is that?
Why that I either by means of my tinder-box or
by gp fire in ge room.

Now that you like I shall have to myself to
having found certain articles which got stamps
being a fine, medicine and some of which I
think not that they are, but I hope them in
my heart of going to my friend.

What else have you got?

I have also that I have found a smaller
green door and a big bone thing a ring is a
fiat a ring. God about medicine the thing some
a long such name of a month cloth such of
my goodbye than somebody that neces
from me like it.

Can you return them to us?

I cannot give things to you to to me so for.
But I have not them all, second some little toys
luncely and this the they are in my house and
therefore are by side to me.

morning I asked my father why he had made the effort to get out of bed, and had then said nothing to me.

He had not got up during the night and neither, for that matter, had anyone else.

The next series of strange events began on a Saturday morning; I remember that it was a Saturday because the whole family was at home. It lasted for a period of six days and started on July 31st, 1971. The reason for my mentioning this date with precision will become clear later.

I happened to go into my bedroom that morning and I noticed a name written in large letters across one of the white-painted panels. It simply said, 'Rob. Webbe'.

It had certainly not been there previously and I could not really imagine that any of my family would write on the walls. I fetched my parents who were intrigued, if not a little annoyed. The name that had been written on the wall was the same as the name signed underneath the automatic message I had received some days earlier. There did not seem much point in erasing it because as the walls were rather dirty anyway it would have made it even more noticeable. And in any case, for all we knew it might reappear again if it was removed. We left the room empty and had a cup of coffee together in the garden.

When, twenty minutes later, my mother walked into the room to have another look at the name, she was rather startled to discover that there was now a second name, also written in pencil, scrawled in large letters about six inches high across another panel on the same wall. This name was 'Hannah Webbe'. Excitedly my mother called my father to come and look at the new name. He was not amused. We knew that nobody in the family had written it—we had all been in the garden.

'Tell Webbe that he is not to write on the walls,' my father instructed.

I fetched a pad of paper and my fountain pen and writing my father's request at the top of the page, concentrated on Robert Webbe's name.

'Indeede I did see your owne fine workes on my familye and

did decide to helpe you by allowing my frendes and allies to sign there names on the wall,' he wrote, as if hurt by the fact that he was being reprimanded.

'You must relize that it is my wall and I am at liberty to write on my owne walls. Youre worke was moste fine and in moste part, very right,' he wrote in defiance.

We were perplexed, not knowing what to do. It seemed that we were about to be invaded by a horde of past villagers who were all going to sign their names on our wall. We really had little choice but to allow events to take their own course. The least we could do was to try to document as carefully as possible anything which might happen.

By lunchtime, about two hours after the appearance of the first name, fifteen more had appeared; most of them seemed to belong to members of the Webbe family. The names were all being written in pencil and soon we found that a pencil lying in the room seemed to be the implement being used as it was becoming increasingly blunt although nobody was using it. What was strangest about this invasion was that if we stayed in the room to watch a name being written, nothing at all happened. The wall had to be out of direct scrutiny it seemed.

Realizing that more names were being added rapidly, we left two sharpened pencils on the bed wondering whether they might be used. They were laid in a crossed position so that it would be easy to detect if they had been moved. However, when we entered the room after luncheon the pencils were still in the same position in which they had earlier been left. Their points were blunted and another two names had been inscribed upon the wall. Once more we all knew that the room had been empty—we had all been together in the dining room.

Up to this point most of the names which had appeared, there now being about twenty, were evidently members of Robert Webbe's family. It seemed, from examination of the signatures, that most of them had been written by different 'individuals' rather than one 'person'. Soon however, names were written which were not of the Webbe family, although they were obviously names associated with the times that the dates below them suggested, for example, 'Lettice Burling 1647', 'Horace Keele 1717', and, 'Jeremiah Tench 1655'.

I was not quite sure whether I wanted to sleep in the room that night and felt apprehensive about what might happen. I told myself that it was unlikely anything would occur as the names seemed only to appear if the room was empty. By the time I had made up my mind to sleep in the room, there were nearly forty names written on its walls.

They were not being produced in any apparently logical sequence or order; they appeared on every conceivable area of the wall, from floor to ceiling, with the exception of the area of wall obscured by my bed. So far most of the names were accompanied by dates ranging right through the seventeenth and eighteenth centuries. (For a full list of the names and a comparison of it with names identifiable from the Parish Registers, see the appendix, pp. 162.) The pencils were lying on a table across the other side of the room; we had even sharpened them once or twice because they became blunt, despite the fact that they were apparently not moving. It appeared that the graphite was being transferred directly from the pencil tips to the walls.

As nothing occurred for the first fifteen minutes during which I lay in bed in the darkened room, I began to relax. Nothing was going to happen while I was present, I reasoned with myself. After about thirty minutes I started to doze off.

I was disturbed a little later by a scratching noise, like a small animal trying to get out of the room. I lay quite still in bed, straining to hear what had aroused me. I could definitely hear a very faint scratching noise coming from the opposite end of the room, but almost as soon as I began to listen to it, it stopped, leaving me wondering if it had been my imagination. I heard another scratch and quickly switched on the light to see what was happening. From my bed I could see nothing odd—the pencils were still on the table across the room—and nothing was disturbed. I got up and walked towards the area from where I thought the scratching sound had emanated.

Something had been written on the door. It was not a name,

but a short piece of verse signed by 'Rob:Webbe', and dated 1733. Without stopping to even read it, I rushed agitatedly upstairs and got my parents out of bed to look at it.

Zeano hearing a young
man speake two frely
says for this reson we
have two ears and one tongue
because we should hear
much and speke litle.

It appeared to have been written by Robert Webbe in his now easily identifiable handwriting. I wrote in ink underneath it the date on which it had appeared, as I was also now doing with all of the signatures, July 31st, 1971. After that incident the night passed uneventfully and the next morning there were no new signatures.

Instead, there was something even more intriguing.

My mother came downstairs and decided to go through the dining room into the kitchen to heat the kettle and make tea for breakfast. Passing through the dining room she noticed a sheet of paper placed on the breakfast table in the position that I usually occupied. As she had set the table the previous evening herself, she knew that it had not been there then.

On closer examination she discovered that it appeared to be a fly-leaf from an old book. Although it had no printing on it, it seemed to be about the size of an average book page. On one side of this sheet of paper was written exactly the same verse as had appeared on the wall the previous evening, with exactly the same mis-spellings and in the same handwriting.

On the reverse side of it was inscribed, in a different hand-writing, 'Thomas Coas write this on the last day of July 31, 1791.'

Was this a coincidence? The date on which the verse on the door appeared had been July 31st, 1971, so that all the figures in the date were identical, except that the numbers in the years were in a different order.

The origin of the piece of paper was unknown. Certainly nobody had ever seen it before.

That morning I decided to ask Robert Webbe, through automatic writing, the origin of this sheet of paper.

'The page was taken from one of my books. I have given it to you and it will not go from before your eyes. I am doing much worke on my familye for you but do nothing for it for two days or I stop. I am always here,' was his answer.

From August 1st, strange events not only continued, but also intensified, and a new phenomenon began to emerge. The names continued to appear in their dozens, as if there was some spirit convention taking place in the room, and all the guests were signing a room-size 'guests' book'. Many of the names were being written in places where it was quite impossible for any human hand to have written them. Some were compressed so far into corners that people later inspecting the wall have been unable to get their hands in, let alone write a signature. Others were written in perfect writing on the ceiling, or on the cornices; some were written upside down with apparent ease. Occasionally someone would enter the room and discover a half-completed name which would not be finished until after the intruder had left the room.

By the time there were more than two hundred signatures covering the walls, my father invited to the house a friend with whom he worked. Early in the afternoon of August 1st, 1971, William Nicholas, an architect, arrived, not knowing quite what to expect. I do not know if he saw what he expected, but here is his memorandum of what happened during the time that he was at Queen's House:

'Being a friend and professional colleague of Derek Manning, and having on numerous occasions expressed an interest in the extraordinary events surrounding his family, it was not without some inner feeling of excitement and expectancy that I set out to Linton early one afternoon. This visit was prompted by an invitation to witness with my own eyes the alleged culmination of several hours hard work put in by some unknown agency.

This agency was supposedly the erstwhile spirit/essence, energy or 'what-you-will' of one Robert Webbe, a former owner and resident of Queen's House, the destination of my visit. Robert Webbe had been selflessly employed in an apparently pointless task of collecting together a vast amount of signatures. These had been culled from persons long since deceased, and generously applied to various parts of the panelled wall surface.

'Having hurried over, anxious not to miss anything, it was surprising to find the complete lack of excitement and utter calm which pervaded the house. They had all, of course, been living within the environment of scientifically inexplicable, and therefore strange events, for years.

'I was taken into Matthew's bedroom and shown the multitude of very interesting signatures which decorated the whole of one and a part of the other adjoining wall.

'These writings, executed with precision and care, using a black pencil, stood out clearly on the white painted wall.

'Furthermore, Matthew had marked each and every appearance with coloured ink, thus recording date and order of arrival.

'Having carefully examined the signatures I was accompanied by the entire household into the sunlit gardens, it being explained that the phenomenon did not and would not occur whilst the wall was under direct scrutiny. A pencil was left, however, hopefully on the bed.

'Some seven to ten minutes later we returned to find that another signature had been newly added.

'This was then, and still is, one of the most interesting and mystifying direct experiences of my life. I am grateful that I was given the opportunity of being witness to this extraordinary event.'

During the afternoon of August 1st, another page of an old book was found lying on the stairs as if it had dropped out of nowhere—maybe it had. It was the same size as the fly-leaf which had been discovered earlier that day, and it seemed likely that both pages had been extracted from the same book. Again nobody had ever seen this piece of paper before. This time, however, it was the title page of a book entitled.

Six Discourses on the following subjects:

I. The use of the Law.
II. The Insufficiency of Creature etc., and the All-sufficiency of CHRIST.
III. The effect of the Grace of God upon the Hearts and Lives of Professors.
IV, V, VI. The Parable of the Sower.

By the Rev. Samuel Hicks, Rector of Wrestlingworth in Bedfordshire,
London: Printed for the author by J. and W. Oliver in
Bartholomew Close, near West Smithfield:
And Sold by G. Keith, in Grace Church
Street; E. and C. Dilly in the Poultry,
and by Messrs. Merril in Cambridge.

It seemed likely that the book had been purchased originally in Cambridge but how, we wondered, were these pieces of book connected with the graffiti on our walls?

That same afternoon my mother had another shock awaiting her. On entering her bedroom, she found the covers of the double bed pulled back diagonally across the mattress as if someone had been sleeping in the bed and had left it unmade. Yet she remembered quite distinctly that earlier in the day the bed had been properly made—in fact it was her habit that the bed should always be made before breakfast. The pillows from both sides of the bed were pushed, roughly up against the headboard and still bore the marks of depression from where someone had been recently lying in the bed, propped up by them. Furthermore the sheets and the blankets were thoroughly ruffled, as was the mat which lay on the floor next to the bed.

None of us knew quite what to do, so we laughed, which was what we had learned to do during earlier poltergeist attacks, and remade the bed. We had decided long ago that being frightened merely made matters worse; also we knew from experience that we would not be physically hurt, which is why probably many people would have been frightened, faced with a similar situation.

The names, by now numbering about three hundred, continued to fill the wall of the downstairs room. We tried to live as if nothing extraordinary was happening.

The following day a third page materialized, apparently from the same book as the previous two pages. This time it was discovered outside the door of my parents' bedroom by my father. The text on the page seemed almost to be a message to us, from Robert Webbe.

'Gentle Reader,' it began.

'Lend me a chair, and I will sit down and talk a little with you. If my company proves unseasonable, or my discourse unsavoury, you may be relieved from both by a single cast of your eye. No longer I continue talking, than whilst you continue looking upon me. My visit will be long or short, just as you please; only while it lasts, it should be friendly. I have no flattering words to give you, nor any alms to ask of you ...'

It was almost as if he was saying that if he frightened us, or we did not enjoy his company, then he would leave. Our only concern, and it applied more to my parents than myself, or my brother and sister, was that Robert Webbe should not become a dominating or controlling force in the household. It was becoming clear that he was gaining power, or perhaps strength, because we now started to detect unmistakable smells in certain areas of the house which were obviously not being caused or produced by any of us. One of the most noticeable odours was that of very strong pipe tobacco smoke which could often be smelled on the staircase. This we knew had an 'external' origin as nobody in the family smoked. Other scents which occasionally wafted across a room included a smell of musty old books, a spicy smell, a smell of lavender-like perfume, and a pungent smell of halitosis. It is perhaps not difficult to imagine that one hears a bump or a knock, but smells are harder to dismiss.

On August 3rd, I received another message in automatic writing from Robert Webbe concerning the signatures on the wall:

'I must explayne to you that I have not completed my many wordes. Do nothing for them still and I shall continue. Indede I did have no realisation of my many friends allies and familye. You must apreciate that I finde it very difficult to do much worke being somewhat infirm in bodily health. Some of these names are names I have written by me and methinks there are many more. I even knowe of halfe of a thousand of such names. Some of them are people who have died on the place when 'twas that of the physick in 1363 and I knowe them not. I shall do my writing for three days more while you watch them before your eyes.'

These messages in their rather quaint form of English amused us and we joked over them, calling Robert Webbe a 'bumpkin' on one occasion because he seemed so simple to us. Evidently he resented being teased and it appeared that he could hear what we were saying about him while we were in the house, because the message I received the following day showed that he was annoyed with us:

'I am continuing still my worke but this day my legs have been so troublesome. I had to rest in the soft bed but I will but wander from my roome except I muste warlke on myne stairs. I must warne you that I shall do nought against you ever but the others frustrate me not a little. I shall not do any action on their behalf but I obey your orders. If your family continue to be so frigtened I must make my presence knowne to all asundry. They do not control me or even less knowe me. I shall continue my worke and you are in my highest esteem. The pages are myne and I give them to you. Take heed of my wordes and taunt me not in any way.'

By now it was becoming clear that as far as Robert Webbe was concerned, the house belonged to him, and not to us. We were strangers. Furthermore, he seemed to regard himself rather than my father as the master of the house. For some unknown reason though, it seemed that I could do no wrong as far as he was concerned. Maybe it was because he realized that I was his only link with the 'outside' world, and that if I cut him off he would be excommunicated again.

The names were still appearing on the walls, and by now Webbe had been engaged in this exercise for nearly five days. He had written,

'I even knowe of halfe of a thousand of such names.'

If he was really intent on collecting five hundred signatures, it looked as though his time was rapidly expiring. At least another one hundred were required in order to make a total of more than 'halfe of a thousand'.

To facilitate the cataloguing or photographing of these signatures at a later date, my father had lettered each panel involved from 'S' to 'Z', while I numbered each name as it appeared. In one case, a large printed 'T' which my father had applied to the wall was incorporated in the signature of one of the 'spirits', Thomas Bucke.

Six days after the writing on the walls had begun, August 5th, was the date by which Robert Webbe claimed that he would have assembled the remaining names to make a total of five hundred. By the morning of that date he would have to produce another eighty signatures in order to complete his assignment on time. By the early evening that day I reached 503 on my numbering system. I sat down with paper and pen and asked Robert Webbe if he had now completed his task.

'I have now finished my worke although methinks I can indever to fynd some more names soon. My legs are so mightye bad and I am forced to retire to my bed often. Soon you may perchance to see me at night but I do wander around my house especially upon the staircase. I am moste happy now and I must go to see my good man Robert Moore soon for some provisions'.

From that time on, the main flow of signatures was stemmed, although at a later count it was discovered that at least another twenty names had been added after we thought they had ceased. Since that time, however, there have been virtually no more additions to this apparent catalogue of departed village inhabitants.

Several of the people called upon by Webbe seem to be illiterate; for example, in Webbe's own handwriting would appear the words, 'Richard Blacke', and underneath would be written, 'His mark', and it would be signed with a cross.

Other signatures were followed by a word which would describe their occupation, such as 'Edmund Keene, Rector 1777', 'William Clarke ye Rector of Hadstocke 1715', or 'Thomas the tailloure 1495'. Another name with an interesting piece of information attached to it appeared on the wall, suggesting that maybe Queen's House had been occupied by other Webbes, before Robert Webbe. It read, 'Henry Webbe my house 1678.'

Yet another interesting name which appeared on the edge of the door read, 'Hugh Dandes, minister 1797'. An elderly gentleman, whose family had lived in Linton since the time of Robert Webbe, and whose consuming interest was local history, recognized the name as that of a past Methodist minister of Linton at about that time. Later this fact was verified when an old ivy-covered gravestone in a corner of the local Methodist chapel graveyard was discovered and cleaned up.

The names had smothered a complete panelled wall, a door, and had spread around the two adjacent walls; they were scrawled on the cornice, the skirting boards, and towards the end, when space was hard to find, on the ceiling.

We could never quite understand the relevance of the dates which appeared with the names (and every name had a date), because they did not seem to be dates of birth or death, as far as we could tell. A good example was the name 'Oliver Cromwell 1643' which was written on the door. His dates were 1599 to 1658. His name was the only one belonging to a famous person, although it need not have been *the* Oliver Cromwell. (For example, there are quite a few William Shakespeares in the Stratford parish records from the fourteenth century on, apparently.) The only explanation for the relevance of the dates is that perhaps they refer to the year in which the person concerned entered the house during their lifetime. The dates range from 1355 through to 1959, although the great majority of them are seventeenth- and eighteenth-century dates.

Maybe more interesting than the names and dates are several short pieces of verse which also appeared on the walls at the same time, each piece being signed by 'Rob:Webbe'.

The first piece, referring to 'Zeano' is really a quotation, actually made by the Greek philosopher, Zeno, who was born about 500 BC, rather than a piece of verse. The next lines which we found could be interpreted as a description of how Webbe saw himself:

A harmless lambent fire
A mistaken phantom.

The remaining pieces of verse were, we thought at the time, placed on the walls with the intention of intimidating us, especially as they all appeared after the piece of automatic writing from Webbe which expressed annoyance with the rest of the family. He wanted to assert himself as being in control of the house, we thought. He rejected my father as master of the house because, as far as he was concerned, it belonged still to him and not us. He wanted to get his own way by threatening us; this we learned later was how his mentality worked. He was used to always getting his own way, nobody questioned his authority. When we arrived in the house challenging his dominance and ownership in his opinion, he reverted to threats and intimidation. All the other verses seemed either to be a description of how he saw himself, or more interestingly, how he saw us.

Doubt's the worst Tyrante of a generous mind
The cowards Ill who dares not speke his fate,

appeared next, to be followed by a rather macabre sentence which read,

The dead are only Happy.

The fifth piece of verse was more philosophical and in the vein of the first piece, and later we found it to reflect quite strongly the mentality which Webbe revealed,

> Seeing aright we see our Woes
> Then what avails us to have eyes?
> From ignorance our Comfort flows,
> The only wretched are the wise.

The next verse appeared one afternoon, placed conspicuously above my bed; it seemed to have been placed there with the intention of instilling fear into the occupant of the bed, who happened to be myself.

> Terror froze up his hair, and on his face
> Show'rs of cold sweat rolled trembling down apace.
> Aghast he wake'd and started from his bed.

The final piece to appear was for me the most interesting and mysterious,

> I had a friend that loved me
> I was his soul: He lived not but in me.

Those were the only selections of verse to appear during the time of the writing on the wall, and they are interesting in as much as Robert Webbe has never repeated this apparent penchant for verse in any of his automatic writings. The source of these verses has never been successfully traced, but I think it highly unlikely that they were actually composed by Robert Webbe.

It seemed evident by the end of the first week of August, 1971, that he was here to stay—in fact, had he ever left the house?

# Two: 'This is myne house. Myne house and myne all.'

Linton, by modern standards, is a large village but during the eighteenth century it was a small market town similar to many other East Anglian towns which had prospered during the boom in the wool trade of earlier years. It was more populous than many of the surrounding villages because it attracted families who would settle, hoping to find fortune with the opportunities of increasing trade. These families flourished and expanded as the village prospered with the growing wool trade; ultimately they all declined as the trade shifted away from East Anglia to the Cotswolds with the dawning of the Industrial Revolution.

Robert Webbe was one of many traders who profited from flourishing business at the beginning of the eighteenth century and, perhaps fortunately for him, he died before his prosperity and wealth began to decline, as it undoubtedly would have done if he lived another ten years.

Linton is now a gangling village, sprawled along a High Street faced with timber-framed buildings, gabled houses, and pargeted cottages which decorate both sides of the River Granta. This river was once filled with clear, fast-running water, stocked with trout. It is now a murky, lethargic river snaking slowly through the middle of Linton. One memento of a time long passed is an old fire hook on a pole, suspended from an old cottage wall in the High Street, which was once used for pulling burning thatch from houses.

Behind the village is the protective presence of the chalk-strewn Rivey Hill, one of the highest points in Cambridgeshire as it rises four hundred feet above sea level.

Except that the nucleus of the village has now been edged

with estates of modern houses, it has hardly altered since Robert Webbe lived here.

As it was obvious that Robert Webbe had been stimulated into action, it seemed an opportune moment to devise a series of questions to ask him about his life, his house, and his family, and to read what his replies, through automatic writing, would be.

Gradually a montage was built up, based on information which Webbe supplied, of life in an eighteenth-century country town.

The first question I asked him, on August 18th, 1971, as I assumed that it would interest him, was,

'Who built the front of the house, and how much did it cost?'

'My house was bilt by one William Crutchley a builder of some repute from Saffron Walden for a goodley sum of two hundred and fifty pounds. My house was started ye November ye 1730 and completed ye July 1731. I died in 1733 from my troublesome legs.'

This was of great interest because on a lead hopper head at the side of the house are the initials 'W.C.' and a date 1731. The reference to his legs was something which was repeated almost unfailingly every time I communicated with Webbe, although this had been the first time that he wrote anything which suggested that he was aware that he had died.

Next I asked him what his occupation was.

'I was a trader of grain of ye Butchers Rowe of Lynton and receeved near seven hundred pounds each year. The half guinea was for payment of a sadle for my horse and some provisions from goode Robert Moore. You will find me close to ye Church on ye southe side. I go and I come.'

After this short time it was clear that Robert Webbe was aware that he was no longer physically alive as he referred to himself and his life in the past tense. His memory seemed quite clear, despite the fact that no Butchers Rowe existed in Linton in 1971. Who was I to say that it had not existed in 1731?

The reference he made to a 'half guinea' made no sense to

any of us to begin with. Then suddenly we associated it as being connected with another strange incident which had occurred a few weeks previously and for which at the time we blamed the poltergeist. My sister had placed a fifty pence piece inside a wooden puzzle money-box and later discovered that it had vanished. We were all naturally accused of the theft of the coin, and we all denied it. Needless to say, she was rather upset.

Not many days later a fifty pence piece, which we assumed to be the same one, appeared on the front door mat. Now Webbe was claiming responsibility, saying that he thought it was a half-guinea, which is what he would have been accustomed to in 1733.

I next asked him to tell me more about his family, who was his father and who were his brothers and sisters?

'My father was Richard Webbe Gent who died in 1703 after falling from his mount. My brothers are Richard and John. My sisters are Sarah and Elizabeth. I was born in 1678 in ye house I now walke. I believe my familye to come from ye vilage of Bartlowe in year of 1565 for purpose of beter trade and land.

'The father of Richard Webbe was Henry Webbe a farmer and his wife Elizabeth. My children were Robert, Richard, John, Elizabeth and Mary. I marryed Mary and my brother marryed Anne. The wife of my poore father passed away and he again married. I have a brother who is not who is also Robert but is dificult for you to understande in your wordes. The name of my mother was Elizabeth who died in ye yeare of our Lord 1719. I did knowe of the name of my son and I am most ashamed at such a deed when I set my eyes upon it. My grandfather supported the fine Oliver Cromwell and even knewe him at Saffron Walden.

'My father rode allong ye Hoggs Lane by side of his house when the bad horse was caused to jump in fright of a dogg and he struck a tree one ye necke dieing four days latter.'

From the information that Webbe had now supplied, it was possible to start constructing a Webbe family tree, which we did, adding to it whenever we were supplied with more information.

I then asked him if he owned any other houses nearby and whether the house was known as Queen's House when he was alive.

'The cottage was myne and leased to my cousin William a shepherd before to Widow Browne and Thomas Tofts. My house had no such name being knowne by me around here.'

As well as information concerning his family, I was also quickly collating information, which may or may not have been accurate, concerning eighteenth-century Linton. Hoggs Lane was certainly no longer in existence, and I was not sure to which cottage Webbe was referring as there was more than one cottage in the vicinity, or at least there must have been at the time that he was alive.

Later we discovered from a local odd-jobbing man who specializes in restoring bricked-up hearths that on a beam over the fireplace of a cottage next door to Queen's House is carved 'Thomas Tofts'.

It was obvious after about two weeks that Webbe was becoming more active, probably because I was somehow providing him with energy. The strange phenomena in the house began to increase.

The bed in my parent's room was often semi-stripped, looking as though someone had been lying in it. Sometimes a light mat at the side of the bed would become askew as if somebody had clambered out of the bed, slipping on the mat.

Pages from what appeared to be an eighteenth-century book would often be found by various members of the household, usually lying on the stairs as if somebody had dropped them there by mistake. They all originated from the same book, and it seemed as though someone was tearing out each page individually.

Then began a new phenomenon, one which seemed to occur more frequently than most of the other strange occurrences connected with the house over the years. Certainly nothing else has been so widely experienced by so many different visitors to the house.

Nobody in our family smokes, nor have they ever done so,

and yet at about this time we began to notice a distinct smell of tobacco smoke; it was the smell of someone smoking a pipe rather than cigarettes. It was first noticed on the staircase, and then in my parents' bedroom and, occasionally, in the hall. One moment it would smell as though someone was smoking in the room, the next moment the air would be quite clear again.

One evening the strong aroma of tobacco smoke was detected in the hallway. I immediately sat down with pen and paper, and asked Robert Webbe if he smoked.

'Indeede I did fanceye a wholesome pipe of toobacco in the evening with myne drink. But not to the fancey of ye poore wife who says it deseases ye mynde. And so off to myne bookes,' he told me.

It was not long after this message in automatic writing that we began to notice another smell—that of old musty books. Again, it was detected in the same places as the tobacco smoke, except that it had also spread to a ground floor room at the front of the house which we used as a study. Suddenly a room would be filled with the smell of old books and then, just as suddenly as the smell arrived, it would vanish again. However, anybody who happened to be in the room would smell the same aroma. We have never managed to trace the origin of any of the strange smells.

Other odours, obviously of the same nature, began to manifest themselves. It seemed that most of them were smells which would be associated with an eighteenth-century household.

It was beginning to appear as though Robert Webbe and his entire household were being brought back to life. It may seem strange to outsiders that we were never really very concerned about it but, having lived previously for so many months amidst the phenomena of a poltergeist, we had lost our fear of phenomena which may seem irrational or frightening to many people. We were intrigued more than anything else and my father always considered that as long as our lives were not dictated or ruled by Robert Webbe, it could do no harm.

Treating it in this way, we all began to regard Webbe more as a 'friend' or person than a ghost.

Visitors to the house would sometimes be greeted by strange smells, almost as if Webbe was using them as a means of greeting them as they entered 'his' house. In addition to the smells of tobacco smoke and old books, we also noticed the scent of lavender and other flowers, a spicy perfume on the landing, and a disagreeable and extremely pungent smell of bad breath which would waft over one's shoulder—almost as if Webbe was standing behind one. These smells were later joined by a very strong stench of rotting fish which often manifested itself if somebody who was not a member of the family entered the house through the front door; there was also an unpleasant odour of rotting meat.

Most of these smells, though, were only experienced in the front area of the house—the section which Robert Webbe built and, apparently, the main area of the house affected by Webbe's 'revival'.

As it seemed that Robert Webbe may have been aware of what was happening in the house, and especially as he was obviously aware of the rest of the family, I decided to ask him some questions about ourselves.

To begin with, I asked him what he thought my name was.

'I believe your name to be Matthew. Indeede I once knewe of one Matthew Hunter of this same village,' he answered.

'What,' I asked him, 'is the name of my sister?'

There was a pause of a few moments before he wrote,

'The name of your sister is one such as Rachel but I must confess I knowe not.'

'Do you know the name of my brother?' I asked him.

'He is knowne by Andrew and is I fancey much like my younge Richard in temperament and age,' he replied.

Next I asked him if he knew the name of my father or my mother, both of whom have names that were not used at the time that Webbe was alive. Interestingly he was unable to give the correct answer to either.

Of my father, he wrote,

'His name know I not of but could perchance be Daniel. I even knowe one Daniel Bittin of Lynton.'

'What is the name of my mother?' I asked.

'It would tickle my fancey to have her name Elizabeth but I do knowe not. She is a goodley woman to my floor but I cannot walke on sticksome boarding.'

I then wrote down on a sheet of paper,

'The names of our family are Derek, Valerie, Matthew, Rosalind, and Andrew. Our family name is Manning.'

There was a few minutes gap as I sat waiting for a reply from him in automatic writing.

'I did knowe some of ye names but not all, I have never heard of Derik or Valeree,' he told me.

The reference to my mother being a 'goodley woman' but making it difficult for Webbe to walk on 'sticksome boarding' was amusing. My mother had recently varnished the boarded floor of the landing, at about the time that Webbe had become active. It seemed silly to think of this ghost getting its feet sticky!

I then asked Webbe whether he saw the furnishings of the house as they were in 1733, or as they were in 1971. His answer was rather interesting, as was a 'conversation' I had with him later concerning electric light switches:

'Indeed I do and some of them are very new. The handles of the new chest in myne room did tincle as I layed on the bed. I fancey the table at bottom of the stairs which I have taken the liberty of writing onn. The bench in my parlour I like but 'tis some clumsy. I like ye delicate art such as ye picture of my Lady in the front room. Too I like ye chares in ye parlour.'

Some months after this communication another strange incident occurred for which Webbe took responsibility. On April 2nd, 1972 my mother found a lighted candle in one of our brass candlesticks placed in the middle of the floor in the groundfloor cloakroom. She was a little dismayed in case any more candles should light themselves near curtains or furnishings, and I was asked to tell Robert Webbe not to light our candles.

'Have you lit the candles?' I wrote down on a sheet of paper, intending to reprimand Webbe for being carelesss. Why he

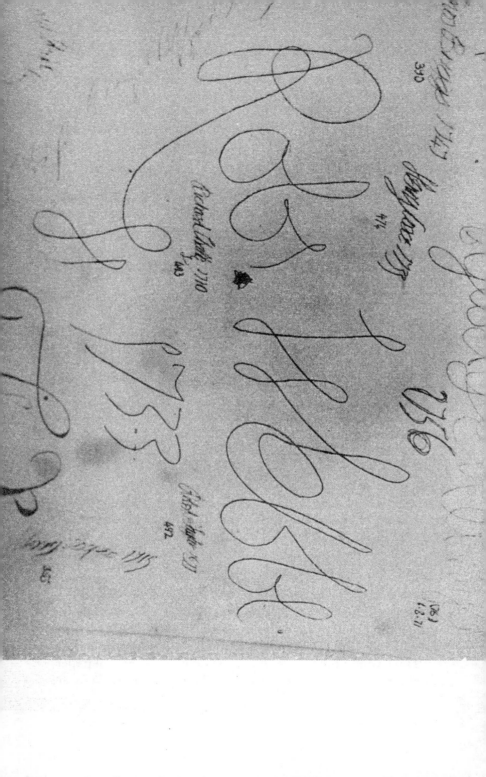

1. The house as it was at the beginning of the century. This is probably how Webbe remembers his house.

2. A view of the rear of the house in which Robert Webbe was born.

3. The bed in my parents' bedroom which became a focal point for Webbe's attention. On several occasions my father felt that Robert Webbe was also in the bed at night. The chest with the handles that 'tincel' can also be seen.

4. The staircase where I met Robert Webbe for the first time. He was standing at the top of the stairs as I stood at the bottom in the same position from which this photograph was taken.

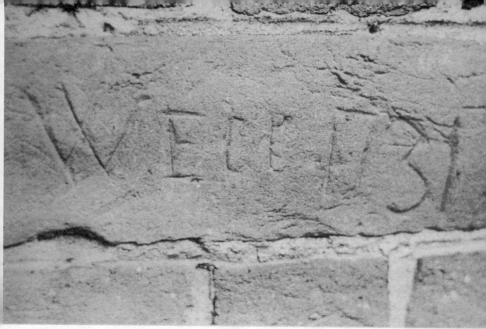

5. The name 'L. Webb 1731' which aroused my interest in the history of the house. This would seem to have been inscribed by Robert Webbe's son, John who was sixteen years old at this time.

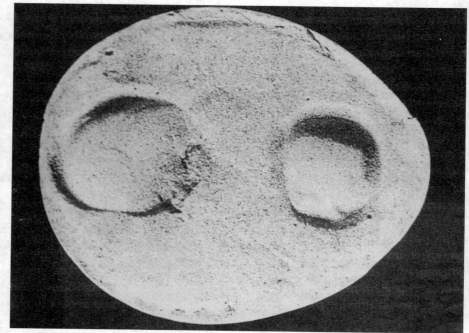

6. The plaster cast of the footprint left in the sand by Robert Webbe.

should want to place a candle on the cloakroom floor, we could not think.

'I do not lite ye candel. My servant Beth shall lite it,' he informed me.

It seemed that there were really more people than just Robert Webbe at work now, if we were to believe all that he told us. It seemed he still had his servants working for him.

'I can save you a lot of bother with you having to light your candles,' I told him. 'Go into your bedroom and stand by the door entering the landing' I instructed.

'I shall have to walke and strayne my poor legs to walke from ye parlour to mine bedchamber,' he complained. 'Happen I can return to fetch my snuff newe from Robert Halls.'

'If you now look on the wall you will see a white round box on the wall,' I told him, referring to the light switch in terms I hoped he might understand. 'On this box is a square object which you can press down.'

There was a gap of several minutes until he wrote automatically,

'Although I am now in ye same place I can perceive no such box.'

'There is a box. Look hard,' I insisted.

'I say there is no box. There has ne'er beene such a box and not shall there be even so longe as I sit on ye dunghill. Hey ho old sow.' Webbe had apparently gone as I could no longer make him write anything automatically.

I found it interesting that as far as the interior of the house was concerned, Webbe was perfectly able, apparently, to see anything which he understood or was familiar with. He described quite correctly furniture and a painting which were in the house, but was unable to see a light switch which was quite definitely on the wall, and which was just as physical as the furniture he saw. Obviously, he knew nothing of electricity and was therefore unable to visualize or comprehend a light switch. If I insisted that there really was such a switch, but that he was not looking properly, he became irate!

When I next managed to get him to continue writing, after

he had calmed down, I asked him if he liked what had been done in our house, referring to the decoration which had been carried out.

'This is myne house. Myne house and myne all,' he insisted. 'I perceeve a funsome shiney gold candle holder in my stairs which does tickle myne fancey not a little. A pretty lite.'

What he was writing was becoming even more intriguing because there was no candle holder where he claimed to be able to see one. There was, however, a big electric light fitting made of polished brass with candle shaped electric light bulbs in it. Clearly he was referring to this.

He could see ordinary candlesticks and candles, but was unable to see an electric light switch. If the two were combined though, he could see it. We always wondered whether, if we substituted the candle-like bulbs for ordinary bulbs, he would still be able to see the fitting.

All this talk about candles seemed to make him even more aware of the candles in holders that were already in the house— a few days later a burning candle was again discovered on the floor of the groundfloor cloakroom.

'Did you light our candles?' I asked him again.

'This I must admit to having being done. I shoulde expres my gratitude for you giving to me in my roome these fine candles which are so much better than those that I have. These candles make so little smoke.'

Obviously Webbe was still used to eighteenth-century tallow candles which doubtless emitted black smoke when lit.

'Why did you place one candle in the water closet,' I asked him, taking care to refer to the cloakroom as a water closet in case he did not comprehend the word cloakroom.

'I know not the WATER closet you tell me of but I did place one of my candles in my servery which was lacking in ye same,' I was told.

The room which we assumed had always been a lavatory or cloakroom had obviously been used as a servery while Webbe was alive, and the room which we now used as a study must have been his dining room.

With this new information about the layout of the house as it had been in 1733, we began to investigate the cloakroom, or servery as Webbe described it, and the study. We decided that what he said was really quite logical.

On either side of the fireplace in the study is a recess, but each is very different in appearance. The recess farthest from the cloakroom is highly decorative and has moulded shelves, is semi-circular in shape and has a false, domed ceiling; the recess on the opposite side of the fireplace, next to the cloakroom, is much larger, is rectangular and rises from the dado rail up to the cornice beneath the ceiling. Within the recent past this had been converted to a shelved cupboard. However, on closer examination, we discovered that at some time it had indeed opened into the cloakroom at a juncture which coincides with another contemporary eighteenth-century cupboard in the corner of the cloakroom.

It seems quite feasible that at one time, before these cupboards were built, there was a hatch in existence, and the cloakroom would then have been used as a servery.

Over the following months from April to September, 1972 the incident with the lighted candle on the cloakroom floor was repeated three times, until it reached what I think was probably a peak, as far as candles were concerned.

On the last occasion that a lighted candle was found, I again asked Robert Webbe why he had lighted one of our candles.

'A fine candle that smokes not. And who can see in such dark. So I lite it.'

I decided that I would tease Webbe merely to see what would happen.

'If you cannot see you should open your eyes,' I wrote on the paper.

'Indeed you are a moste funsome jester. Zeano hearing a young man speke says for this reason we have two eyes and two ears that we may see much and speke little.'

He seemed to have missed the point I was trying to make, so I told him,

'You speak too much and see too little.'

'You are a scoundrelle such as I have not heard since myne sonne was so free tonged. You shoulde go to ye stockes with blessed Barnarde. You taunt me scoundrel. I go.'

He signed his name hastily and I was unable to get him to write anything more. It seemed that I had upset him. I felt that he was not so much upset about me teasing him, as the fact that I was making fun of Robert Webbe who was a Gentleman. In the eighteenth century the title of 'Gentleman' was merely passed from father to eldest son upon the father's decease. Property was frequently acquired simply because it provided an opportunity to rise up the social ladder; with the ownership of property came the chance of becoming a 'Gentleman'. The typical English country Gentleman, such as Robert Webbe, is portrayed excellently in the verse by Soame Jenyns on Dr. Samuel Johnson:

'Religious, moral, generous, and humane
He was,—but self-sufficient, rude and vain;
Ill-bred and overbearing in dispute,
A scholar and a Christian,—yet a brute.'

Maybe he had a guilty conscience about the candles that he had lighted belonging to us, or maybe he wanted to show us why he preferred our smokeless candles to his own, because that evening an obviously very old, but unused, tallow candle was found lying on the staircase. Nobody had ever seen it before, and nobody knew from whence it had come.

We decided that it must have originated from the same place as the sections of the book. I thanked Webbe for the candle, but he could not be made to write anything. He was still suffering from hurt pride.

Occasionally over the ensuing weeks we would find parts of the book left lying on the stairs, or on the bed in my parents' bedroom. We found that we were gradually assembling the whole volume although it was still without covers.

At about this time I had a friend to stay whom I had not known for very long. We were both at school together but we were in different houses which meant that he had not experienced the poltergeist phenomena of the preceding months. Obviously, he had heard stories about what was going on. He admitted that he was rather sceptical—he is that type of person and is now an army officer. He had not long been in the house when Webbe decided to introduce himself.

'I had not known Matthew very long at this time, and when he showed me these pieces torn from an old book, supposedly left lying on the stairs by the ghost of Robert Webbe, my reaction was, naturally, sceptical,' my friend later wrote.

'Matthew showed me around the house, and after seeing the ground floor rooms we climbed the back stairs and looked at all the first floor rooms.

'When we arrived at the top of the main staircase I was amazed to see that in the short time it had taken us to walk round the house, more pieces of paper torn from a book had appeared on the stairs, despite the fact that I knew for certain that the stairs had been clear before we started out. Matthew was with me all the time, and at that time there was no one else in the house.'

It took nearly two months for the entire book to be deposited in pieces down the stairs. It turned out to be two volumes bound in one cover, the first entitled, *The Christian World Unmasked, Pray Come And Peep*, and a second volume, to which I have previously referred, called, *Six Discourses*.

The interesting thing about the book was that it had no date in it anywhere, although books invariably state at the beginning the year in which they were first published. It seemed fairly clear that although the book was definitely old, it was not contemporary with Robert Webbe if he had died in 1733. It looked as though it was probably printed towards the end of the eighteenth century rather than the beginning.

It puzzled us for quite some time, until we began to notice that certain of our belongings had apparently vanished in the house.

Then things began to fit together.

# Three: 'When this you see Remember me and bear me in your mind'

In 1970, my father had acquired a complete set of four seventeenth-century Linton tradesmen's tokens, three being farthings and the other a halfpenny. They were not particularly valuable but were of considerable local interest.

A token was an unofficial coin used in lieu of the official currency when there was insufficient coinage for normal daily use. Usually they looked like ordinary coins made of copper or brass, bearing the imprint of the tradesman who paid them out in place of official coinage. They were issued on the understanding that they could be redeemed for silver coin of the realm on demand. Between 1649 and 1672 over ten thousand different tokens were issued by tradesmen and local authorities in nearly every town and large village in England and Ireland.

The first of the Linton tokens bore the name 'Robert Moore', and was dated 1667; the second was inscribed, 'John Byttin 1657', the third was issued by Robert Halls in 1667, and the fourth carried the name 'John Harvey', and was not dated. Unfortunately the tokens do not tell one what trade was pursued by the merchants who issued them.

The four tokens were kept in a large glass-fronted cabinet next to the fireplace in the sitting room where anybody could look at them.

One evening I decided that I would tell Robert Webbe about these tokens and see if he knew anything about the tradesmen who had issued them, although I realized that they had all been issued before Webbe was born, in 1678. However, family businesses continued for many generations at that time, and as the eldest son always seemed to be given the same Christian name as his father, the chances were that Webbe would know the children of these tradesmen, who probably ran businesses themselves by 1730.

'We have in the front room four tradesmen's tokens belonging to Robert Moore, John Byttin, Robert Halls and John Harvey,' I told Webbe. I was going to ask him also if he could tell me anything about these gentlemen, but before I got a chance, he had seized my hand to write.

'I must use such tokens as you can not spend them. If I see them I can use them to pay my provisions for my goode man Rob: Moore.

'This is very fine news. I can now paye for my candels and by some lotions. These are goodley men. I must by some tallow soon.'

'Was Robert Halls a man who made lotions?', I asked him.

'Indeed he was an apothecary and made a fine herb remedy for younge Richard last winter when he was ill of ye cheste. A goodley clever man I fancy.'

'Who was John Harvey then?' I wanted to know.

'His premises were situatted at Butchers Row next my shoppe and he makes ye beste candles of all Lynton I fancy. There are five of his candels in my front room,' he told me.

I had discovered, therefore, that Moore was apparently a grocer (later on Robert Moore became one of the main characters in Webbe's narratives), Halls was what we now know as a chemist, and Harvey was a candle maker.

After Webbe had said that the tokens were of no use to us although he could use them, we kept a watchful eye on the cabinet to ensure that they stayed there, although we really had no reason at that time to suspect that they might vanish, as Webbe did not seem to be in the habit of removing objects.

The tokens stayed where they were for a number of weeks and it was not until everybody had forgotten that I had mentioned them to Webbe that it was noticed they were no longer in the cabinet. It was over two months since, through automatic writing, I had been told about the tradesmen.

My father was obviously annoyed that he had lost the tokens and I was told to retrieve them from Webbe. As might have been expected, he informed me that I could not possibly use them, so he may as well keep them.

'But they belong to my father and he is now very angry,' I told him, realizing that I was powerless to do much.

The next day my mother found them scattered over the floor of my parents' bedroom whereupon they were returned safely to their rightful position.

At that point in January, 1972, Webbe seemed to go quiet and he produced no more automatic writing—in fact we wondered if he had returned to where he had originated.

I think that he was merely saving his energy for the next strange incident which he provoked.

I remember that it was early one morning in the late summer of 1972. I also remember wondering how my mother had managed to drop a small loaf of bread on the stairs—she is not in the habit of doing such things.

I went to pick it up and before I had even touched it properly, I pulled my hand sharply away. It was not an ordinary loaf of bread because it had just given me an electric shock.

It was not really so much an electric shock but the type of 'static' shock that one sometimes receives from a car door, or a door handle after one has walked over nylon carpet. The shock was made worse though by fright.

Quite obviously it was not a loaf which had been dropped by anybody in the house, and I kicked it gently. It rolled over and when I knelt down I could see that embedded in it were complete grains of wheat and even pieces of chaff. Furthermore it seemed quite burned on the top and round the sides, as if it had been cooked in an open range hearth rather than a modern gas or electric cooker.

I reached my hand out gingerly to pick it up and heard another crack as a spark, like static electricity, jumped between my fingers and the loaf. I made a grab for it, picked it up and could have sworn that it was giving me a prickling sensation in my hand, although that may well have been only a psychological reaction.

The loaf was quite cold—it had not been freshly baked.

Strangest of all was the fact that it was as hard as concrete, and about as heavy.

It seemed so odd, finding this loaf which seemed to have 'dropped in' from a previous time, just lying on the stairs while the sunlight poured in through the windows. It was all so normal and un-ghostly.

I carried the loaf to the kitchen; my mother was sure that five minutes earlier it had not been on the stairs. She had never seen it before and neither had anybody else.

It was placed in a box together with the book and the tallow candle while I sat down with paper and pen to ask Robert Webbe why he had left a loaf lying on the stairs.

He was not particularly forthcoming and all he told me was,

'I must tell you that the same loafe was bakered specially for you by Annie my cooke.'

About three days later an old silver sixpenny piece in mint condition was found on the stairs in the same place as the loaf had been found. It did not belong to anybody in the house, and I could not make Webbe write anything about it.

Even though he was now reluctant to write, he was far from dormant, although at the time he may have seemed so.

It was more than three months later when I went to the chest of drawers in my bedroom to fetch a printed silk scarf only to discover that it was no longer where I remembered having left it.

Straightaway I accused my sister, who flatly denied taking it; my mother did not know where it had gone—she had last seen it in the drawer.

Whilst looking for the missing scarf my mother noticed that two nineteenth-century prints usually hanging on the wall in my parents' bedroom had also vanished.

We all looked at each other and said,

'Webbe!'

I fetched my paper and pen and sat down to tell him that I wanted the missing objects returned, as well as anything else he might have taken without our noticing.

'Nowe that you ask I shal have to profess to having founde certayne articels such for example being a fine neckerchief and

some of which I knowe not what they are, but I keepe themm
in my pockets or give to my friends,' he confessed.

I began to hope that my scarf had not been given to one of
his friends.

'What else do you have?' I wanted to know.

'I have also that I have founde a small waxen doll and a
fyne bone knife a pinne for a hat a fine booke about methinks
one Thomas Jones or some such name a pretty cloth such as
my goodley man John Byttin has never seen the like of.'

As far as I could tell from his descriptions, none of these
objects had been removed from *our* household, but then neither
had any of the other objects that we had found around the house
and for which Webbe claimed responsibility. There was no
reference to the two missing prints.

I asked Webbe to return all the objects belonging to us that
he had taken.

'I cannot give these to you for so many reasons. First I have
not them all, second some tickle myne fancey and thirdlee
they are in my house and therefore are by rite to me,' I was
told.

It was becoming increasingly clear that as far as he was concerned the house still belonged to him. He had paid for it and
we were merely strangers who had moved in without his permission. Therefore anything we brought with us was rightfully his
if left in his house. It seemed that there was going to be a show-
down between Webbe and my father, with the mediator being
myself.

'What have you done with our two pictures?' I began.

'Two mightey fine small pictures for mine parlour, butt shall
have to hyde them for some weeks lest they be found,' he said,
almost as if expecting me to be siding with him rather than
my father.

It was almost as if he was letting me in on his secret and
asking me not to tell my father.

'Where have you hidden them?' I asked him.

'In my secrette hole in ye house. No more can I say. Hidden
with mine moneys.'

'My father is very angry,' I warned him, 'and insists that they be returned immediately.'

Predictably came Webbe's reply,

'This house is mine and I owne all of ye same. Ye father must not telle me what to doe. Stupidd countrey bumpkin such as Barnarde.'

Fortunately we quickly realized where the 'secrette hole' was to which Webbe had referred. It was a small compartment constructed in the floor of my parents' bedroom, the existence of which we were aware, although we did not use it.

We undid the screws which secured the lid and lying in the bottom of the compartment were the two prints. The 'moneys' to which Webbe referred were not there, however.

Robert Webbe, it seemed, was a kleptomaniac. It was beginning to appear that he had been active in the house ever since he had died in 1733. Perhaps nobody else had ever been aware of him. The objects which he claimed to have, as well as those which he had already left for us, had obviously originated from earlier families who had occupied the house. We were now being given their belongings and probably in ensuing decades some other family would be the recipients of certain of our belongings.

The 'apport phenomenon', as we call it, continued spasmodically over the following eighteen months, and then seemed to fade away to a large extent although we did occasionally notice isolated instances of objects vanishing, to be replaced by others. I think that all the apports probably belonged to three or four groups of past occupants of the house. I can only speculate as to the reasons for this—maybe those households all contained somebody with latent psychic abilities who acted as a dynamo for Webbe. It is doubtful, I think, that any of the apports are actually contemporary with him.

Other apports included a green glass bottle neck of about 1770, a taper used for lighting a large number of candles, which was not very old, a pair of soiled white nylon gloves, a piece of iron pyrites, a string of battered plastic beads, an aging cork bung, two inches in diameter, an old nickel silver thimble, a

Earl Bathurst
1519 (71)
3.8.71

6.8.71

John Palmer
1797
270

368

Rich: Potter
272

...Freeman
507 (12)
3.8.71

James Lefebve

340

Thomas Langdon 425

1(19) (124)
3.8.71

Hugh Page
1787
405

William Richardson 1820

Courtenay Partridge
1749

(160)
3.8.71

Thomas Haskell
1835
468

Hampton ...
149
230

Robert Partridge
1696
(199)
4.8.71

diamond-shaped pane of sea-green glass, two more loaves both of which were smaller than the first loaf, a plain well-worn gold ring, an old typewritten letter, a stone in which was embedded a fossilized fern leaf, two cigarettes of a brand which had been discontinued, a second eighteenth-century book, a piece of polished granite, a snuff box in the form of a fish, and a half-bottle of gin.

Almost without exception, these apports were discovered either on the landing or in the vicinity of my parents' bedroom, the staircase, or the hallway.

The fossilized fern leaf embedded in an oval-shaped piece of slate was different, however. I found it lying on my bed on the evening of December 24th, 1971. The fossil was a superb specimen of a complete fern leaf, about three inches in length. On the back of it was scratched 'Rob: Webbe 1733'. My parents were rather more surprised than perhaps I was, because it had appeared while the house had been empty, and we all knew that it had not been on the bed before we had left the house. I asked Webbe about it.

'This is indeed a small gift for the Festive Seasonne. A storey goes with it which is thus: some laborors dug it out ye grounde while diging a trench for the walls of this same house and I believe it to be magick.'

To us the stone did not seem magic and his explanation for it seemed even more spurious. Slate is a stone completely alien to East Anglia, so it is highly unlikely that such a fine fossil should be discovered in this area. I suspect that it belonged to a previous occupant of the house who owned a collection of geological specimens, and that the piece of iron pyrites and the polished granite pebble which later appeared, originated from the same place. Maybe Webbe was not prepared to admit that he had 'stolen' it from somebody, so he made up this story. Why this should be the case I am not sure, because he freely admitted to having taken objects from us.

As Webbe had given me a Christmas present it was decided that we should reciprocate and we soon found a small pottery bowl which I had made at school. Having made this decision we then had a problem—how were we to present it to him?

I informed Robert Webbe that I had left a small gift for him on the stairs, whereupon he replied through automatic writing that he was very pleased and would take it. The pot was therefore left on the stairs at 11.50 p.m. on Christmas Eve and we waited to see what would happen.

When everybody rose the following morning the pot was still sitting on the stairs. We were not too surprised as we really did not expect it to disappear. At least if any member of the family had wanted to remove it as a joke, they had had ample opportunity during the night.

The pot remained all morning and by lunch time had still not gone. At about three o'clock on Christmas afternoon the family, joined by my grandparents and a family friend, entered the sitting room to open our presents, but not before my father had checked the stairs to see if the pot had gone. It had not.

One hour later when we inspected the staircase we found that it had vanished. During that hour nobody had left the room and, had they done so, their absence would have been noticed by everybody else. While nine of us had been opening presents, the pot had apparently been removed.

One of the stranger apports to be discovered at this time was a sheet of notepaper with a typewritten text on it. My mother found it lying on the landing floor one December afternoon in 1973.

The letter was headed with the name and address of a firm of London solicitors by the name of 'Housman & Co.' whose address was '7 New Court, Carey Street, W.C.2'. It read,

'Dear Sir,                                    22nd March, 1948.

*H. H. Denne's Estate*

We thank you for your letter of the 19th inst. enclosing the Insurance Premium renewal form with which we are dealing.

Yours faithfully,

[unclear signature]

G. S. Dixon, Esq., The Hall, Holton-le-Moor, Lincoln.

We were all completely baffled by this strange letter that we had found lying on the floor. We knew none of the names mentioned and we had certainly never dealt with this firm of solicitors, if indeed they existed, which for all we knew was problematical. Nor is anyone with the name of Dixon mentioned in the deeds of the house at any time. From where or whom Webbe obtained the letter remains an unexplained mystery. However I did seek information through automatic writing from Webbe and his reply was as follows:

'Indeed a moste fancifull piece of paper as I see not before with writing such as tyckles myne fancey. I did plucke ye same from myne house . . .'

No more was ever discovered. It seemed that he had been rather struck by the typewriting on it, which obviously he would have never seen while he was alive. Maybe something which was meaningless to us was an object of fascination for him.

The second eighteenth-century book to appear was rather more interesting than the first book, which arrived in pieces. The second one was discovered as a complete book on the landing around Christmas 1973 and it seemed to be closer in date to Robert Webbe himself than the first.

The pages of the book were well worn and covered with scribbling and notes, including several sets of names and initials. The predominant names were 'J. Braddon', 'Thomas Cropp', and a large letter 'W' which was written in exactly the same style as those contained in Webbe's automatic writings. On the back cover of the book was written a short verse, similar in style to those which Webbe had written previously. I cannot say if he owned this book when he was alive, but if he did, he may have written the verse which seemed to be a veiled message from him to us,

When this you see
Remember me and bear
me in your mind.

Another of the apports was a diamond-shaped pane of

sea-green coloured glass which was found on a window sill in the hall. When asked about it Webbe wrote automatically,

'Didst soe tickle myne fancie when I didst see, I must place't in myne pocket. A prettye Greene glasse peece to put on ye handsome tray of myne name. And off so soon to see Daniel Browne for my corn, a mightye fine harvest.'

The messages I was receiving from Webbe increasingly gave the impression that he was reliving his earthly life all the time, as he frequently referred to all the people he had known as if they were still people living normal lives in Linton in 1733. It took some time for us to work out to what he was referring when he mentioned a tray with his name on it. Then we realized that the pane of glass had been found on a stone window sill, onto which my father had had inset, 'Built by William Crutchley in 1731 for Robert Webbe, Esquire'. We had decided to have the inscription placed on the sill after Robert Webbe had initially told us when the house was built and by whom.

A few months later two dried-up cigarettes of Players Navy Cut brand were found lying on the stairs as if they had been dropped there. They were picked up and placed in the box along with the other apports.

Then occurred an event which, retrospectively, I regard as having been probably the peak of the apport phenomenon.

My father collects antique drinking glasses which are housed in a glass-fronted cabinet in the sitting room where they can be easily admired and studied. One evening, on entering her bedroom, my mother saw one of my father's antique drinking glasses standing on top of a coffer.

On closer inspection she realized that it had originated from the glass cabinet in the room below. But the glass was not empty.

It seemed that Webbe had been disturbed in the middle of a drink as nobody else ever removed one of the glasses from the cabinet.

My mother called me up to the bedroom and I could see that the glass was filled nearly to the brim with a brown liquid which looked heavy, with a deposit of sediment in the bottom of the glass. I sniffed it and thought it smelt of port.

When this strange liquid was discovered I fetched my pad and pen and asked Webbe what it was.

'What,' I enquired, 'is the drink that you have left in our glass?'

'It was a fine potionne sold me by mine goode man Daniel Byttin for mine poor legs. Tis of wheat, honney, some fine port and much sugar. I know not what houre glasse you say of,' he answered.

This particular message was of great interest, not because of the fact that we now knew what were the contents of the glass, but because he mistook 'our glass' for 'hour glass'.

Whenever I do automatic writing, I first write down in my own handwriting the question I wish to have answered. I was never quite sure up to this point whether whoever writes the automatic messages actually reads what I have written, or whether they 'hear' me say the question as I think it out in my mind whilst writing it. Obviously the latter was the case as Webbe thought I had referred to an 'hour' glass which was not what I had written, although he may have made this error if he had *heard* me ask the question.

Rather than dispose of this curious new apport down the drain, I poured it into a small screw-top jar. Now it began to change its colour as if it was a chamelion.

Within an hour of it having been transferred from the drinking glass to the jar it had changed its colour from a shade of rusty brown to a shade of deep purple. Nobody had touched the jar and I assumed that it may have altered colour because it was in a sealed container. After a further one hour and a half it had begun to change colour once more and became inky blue. Not only was the liquid changing colour, but so too was the sediment which had not resettled in the bottom of the jar.

When everybody went to bed it was still a shade of blue, and how many times it may have changed colour in the night will never be known. The next morning it was bright grass green.

The jar containing this strange liquid remained on the kitchen window sill for several days changing hue like colours in a rainbow, through shades of yellow, orange, red, brown, purple, blue and green.

One morning when everybody came down for breakfast it was noticed that the jar was empty. All that remained was a very fine layer of brown sediment. The liquid had disappeared as mysteriously as it had arrived.

The curious thing about these apports is that most of them have been found along a certain route, centred around the staircase, and this 'track' coincides with the path along which the smells have occurred. It was also on the staircase that I had first seen Webbe.

None of the apported objects had ever been seen before by anybody and yet I am convinced they are all things which Webbe could have taken from previous occupants over the years. Few of the objects are contemporary with him, and yet neither are they contemporary with us. Nobody has ever seen any of these objects materialize—they are always discovered haphazardly lying on the floor as if dropped by somebody walking through. Why Robert Webbe should want to leave them lying around is difficult to understand, and I really have no explanation.

I think that he has a 'magpie's eye' to a great extent because many of the objects are things which look valuable, although they are not. Maybe Webbe mistook the old white nylon gloves for kid gloves. Certainly nylon was not made in 1733. The string of battered plastic beads had, I should imagine, been thrown away by their owner, and I can imagine that Webbe retrieved them in the belief that they were valuable because they sparkled. He would not have known of plastic—maybe he thought they were stone. Other apports were 'pretty' things— the glittery chunk of iron pyrites, the diamond-shaped pane of green glass, the silver thimble, the gold ring, the silver sixpence, and the curious brass snuff box in the shape of a fish.

How many objects we have 'lost' in return for the objects we have been 'given', nobody knows. I am certain that often articles can vanish and one never thinks about them again, or maybe one does not realize that they are missing until some months later, by which time it is too late to do anything about it. Included on our list of lost property at the time of writing are, however, two silk scarves, the original sketch that I drew of Robert Webbe, and the first handwritten manuscript of this book.

The original sketch that I made of Webbe when I saw him on the stairs vanished from a large bag containing all his automatic writings; fortunately a number of photocopies of the drawing had been made and we still retain those copies.

The original first draft of this book also disappeared from a drawer containing nothing but the two files holding the material. Again, fortunately, there was a photocopy of each page already made.

All the objects which have been found in the house are kept in a well sealed cardboard box, and are rarely removed from the building. The majority of the apports are still with us although we have lost the gold ring, the typewritten solicitor's letter, and the snuff box, which seems to come and go!

These, however, were not the only form of materializations that appeared because Robert Webbe also devised another means of materialization combined with literal automatic writing. This he introduced in April, 1972.

# Four:    '*My minde is moste vexed*'

My mother, who likes things to be thoroughly planned in advance, is in the habit of jotting down on a sheet of paper the meals that she plans to prepare during the forthcoming week. On one occasion in April, 1972, she wrote the days of the week down on one side of an envelope and was called away before she had completed planning the meals. She left the pencil with which she had been writing next to the envelope and was only briefly absent. When she returned she saw, to her dismay, that the envelope was now covered in writing and, studying it a little more closely, realized that the handwriting matched that of Webbe's automatic messages.

He had compiled his own menu against each of the days she had listed on the paper and it now read,

'Wednesday. I would say ye smalle woode doves stuffed with almonde.

'Friday. For this day I fancey Carpe and sause of pea.

'Saturday. A side of tender pig from my man Rob: Moore for 2/2 and spiced stuffing.

'Sunday. For this day have a goodley meal. Perchance ye swanne and pike fillets with ducke purchased from goode Rob: Moore.

From my goode man Rob: Moore some 9d. for a whole fishe.'

Taking another sheet of paper, I sat down and wrote,

'One pound of bacon costs seven shillings and eight pence.'

'This is moste mightey disreputable,' he replied, 'I buy a whole hogg from Rob: Moore for about 7 shilings.'

I decided to enlighten him about food prices in 1972, and wrote,

'One dozen large hens' eggs costs six shillings.'

'I cannot believe this. I had my own foul but eggs cost 2d. only for twelve from Mr. Moore.'

He could hardly believe it when I told him,

'A coat and breeches cost £50, hand-made by a tailor.'

'This is moste distressing. I purchase a fine coate, breeches and stockings and fine hat for £6 in Cambridge,' he wrote.

This provided an interesting insight into his life during the eighteenth century, although I was unable to judge the authenticity of the menus. Such topics became frequent during 'conversations' between Webbe and myself. Often I would sit down if I had nothing to do and ask Webbe what he was doing. Invariably I would get an answer indicating that he still believed he was living in the eighteenth century.

On one occasion Webbe wrote automatically,

'Indeed this verey nite am I to have supper with mine goode man Rob: Moore and his goodley wife. She dost tickle myne fancey if I may so say.'

'What will you have for supper?' I asked him.

'My goode maide Beth doth prepare for us some fine bird with rabitt and sauce of blackberey and fyne wyne.'

I could not persuade him to write any more that night—maybe he had gone away to enjoy his dinner.

On another occasion when I asked what he was doing, he was again going out to eat,

'And so off with goode wyfe Elizabeth to see my goode mann Rob: Moore and a fine lunch two. A fyne pyke and ducke and so on to church. I must see you soone and deliver to you more godes,' he wrote, referring, presumably to further apports.

Later I asked Webbe whether he heard all the noise we made because at that time my father was using an electric drill with sanding disc to remove paint from the walls, and there was also much hammering and banging. It seemed that Webbe's senses did not pick up electric machine noise, but he did complain a little about our speech.

'If I am perchance in ye room I can hear some. You speke bad tongue though I do not understand it.'

I asked him to explain what he meant by 'bad tongue'.

'I mean ye wordes I canot understand and I have never heard the like of before.'

'Which words do you mean,' I enquired.

'There are unfamiliar words like carre and bulbbe but I cannot spell them.'

The fact that he could not spell them was of little consequence—he was unable to spell most words!

'A car is a horseless carriage,' I tried to explain, realizing that he would not know what a car was and that being the closest description I could think of, in terms of a concept which he could understand.

'I have never heard the like of such nonsense for a long time. All carriages must have a horse else they stand still,' he chided.

'Would you like to come to Cambridge in our horseless carriage?' I asked him.

A few moments passed and then he wrote,

'Indeed it would do my poor legs no goode and it is better for me to travel on my tamed lion,' he quipped, thinking that I was joking with him about the horseless carriage.

Telling him that I was not joking, I said that it took us less than twenty minutes to travel to Cambridge in our horseless carriage.

'It takes me some one houre or more across a bad road and much wild land covered in part by wood,' he wrote, as if not knowing quite whether or not I was being serious.

'You can fly to the Mediterranean in three hours,' I told him.

'Indeed I see you are a fine jester,' he wrote, his incredulity stretched to the limit. 'Do not tell me such stories. Perhaps Barnardes' son can ride a cammell,' he mocked.

This was not the first time he had referred in disparaging terms to 'Barnardes' son' and it seemed that this person was some kind of village idiot who amused Webbe because of his stupidity.

'I am not jesting. I tell only the truth,' I said.

'I begin to doubt you,' he replied. 'Indeed I have a tame lion who gards my house while standing on ye roofe.'

Webbe was obviously now merely exchanging what he considered to be one tall story for another!

'It takes only twenty minutes to fly to France,' I informed him.

'This cannot be true. Birds are the only creatures to fly and it takes some three days to cross to France. I cannot believe such ridicule and nonsense.'

On another occasion I informed him that I had just flown back from Canada, and it had taken about six and a half hours to travel three and a half thousand miles. He still did not believe.

'Such nonsense I cannot believe. I cannot believe this I tell you,' beginning to sound as though he was getting upset at my telling 'such stories'.

'Birds are onley creatures to fly. Such nonsense. And where is thys place that is called Canda. canda. Such nonsense. My Mr. Moore will laugh his hat off,' he continued.

From that time on, the 'horseless carriage' became a joke. I could not help getting the impression that he was rather afraid of the thought of a horseless carriage, because each time I mentioned it subsequently he became very serious. It was apparent that he was quite unable to comprehend or accept anything outside his own experience or milieu. The idea of men flying was quite ludicrous as far as he was concerned. Even when I had told him of the names of each member of the family, he had to relate those names he had not heard before to his own experiences, as he also did with the names Matthew and Andrew.

I do not know when daffodils were first introduced into Britain but Herrick who lived between 1591 and 1674 had written in this poem: 'Fair daffodils we weep to see you fade so soon...' Robert Webbe either did not know what they were or he was unable to see them. One morning in the spring of 1972, seeing a large number of daffodils flowering in the garden, I asked him if he had seen them.

'I must confess to [k] no [w] not what you say of. These dafodyls or some such like. Indeede all I perceive from ye windowe is John who dordles with ye carts and the maids and anyone else he sets his eyes upon.'

I could not see from the windows of the house the things that Webbe claimed to be able to see. Obviously, as far as he was concerned, it was still 1733 and when he looked out of the windows he saws the scenes of that time. I could see only gravel and the lawns. Webbe never appeared to have much time for his son John—I think he regarded him as a young layabout because he referred, on a number of occasions, to his wasting time.

Scratched into a well-preserved red brick near a window at the back of the house is the inscription 'J. Webbe 1731'. This must have been inscribed on the brick when the house was only a few months old, and one can imagine the chagrin of Robert Webbe when it was discovered. Ironically it is now listed as being of historical interest in the preservation order on the house.

Time and dates were other topics which Webbe was unable to be precise about and this was revealed when I decided to ask Webbe what day and month it was. Did he really believe that it was still the 1730s, I wondered.

First of all I asked him where he was.

'I am in ye same dining roome for a fine meale of brace of partridge from my goode man Rob: Moore.'

'What day and month is it?' I asked him.

'I shall have to find me out this,' he replied.

There was a wait for a couple of minutes before he started to write automatically a strange sequence of numbers in a row.

'31 1234567
1 2 3 4 5 6 7 8 9 10 11 12        31 1
                                   1

'This sore vexes me not to knowe mine owne time. By mine owne pockett watch I perceive ye houre to be nigh on eight hours. The date must be ye Aprill Seconde of ye yeare 1727.'

Jane Batcher
1835

Harriet Livingstone
1709

(29)   31.7.71

John Munn
1827

Thos. de Parise
1365

496

(119)
2·8·71

In fact the date, maybe coincidentally, *was* April 2nd, but the year was 1972.

'It is not 1727. It is 1972,' I wrote.

'If ye yeare is 1972,' he wrote very slowly, as if puzzling over the problem, 'then I shall be under ye cold stones. It has been ye year of our Lorde 1727 for close on foure monthes. Perhaps you can tell me I am living on ye Church tower with ye Deville'.

It seemed that Webbe strongly believed that he was now living in 1727 despite the fact that the previous year he had written that he died in 1733. I could only conclude that he must be trapped in some kind of postmortal nightmare, unable to leave the house on which he had spent so much of his money, and of which he was so proud. Sometimes he remembered that he was no longer physically alive and at other times he was still trapped in the time at which he died.

Here an image occurred to me. I visualized time as a record being played on a gramophone. The needle moved along the groove and time progressed. If the motor of the gramophone was reversed, one retraced the groove which had already been played and time would be repeated. With Webbe it was as though there was an obstruction in the groove at the point of his death which caused the needle to jump back across the grooves through which it had previously played. Thus Webbe was somehow reliving the final years of his physical life over and over. Sometimes I seemed to communicate with him as the needle reached the obstruction on the surface of the record, and he would be aware that he was now dead, and at other times I would communicate with him after the needle had jumped back again.

This seemed an attractive image and explained to me why Webbe, when asked what the date was, always gave varying dates between 1727 and 1733.

On another occasion when I told Robert Webbe that it had been 1972 for four months he was quite incapable of comprehending this, and retorted in a way he considered to be rude to me.

'I cannot explaine this to you. Our King George came to ye throne in 1714 which makes some

$$\frac{27}{14}$$
13 years.

Do you doubt the Royalle Majesties Reign or are you a bumpkin.'

'I shall inded have to think,' he began.

'One winter in 1721 one John Barnarde took a crossing over ye frozen river in his cart when ye ice snapped because of the thinness of the ice. He dared not move and it snowed fast as he sat in the middle of ye river being not able to move. He sat there for three whole dayes and nites and was fed and clothed by provisions supplied from ye banke, poor man. All ye funsome children did come to throw balls of snow at him.

'A clownish mein. A Voice with rustick sound
And stupid Eyes that ever watched the ground.
The ruling Rod, the Fathers forming care,
And his supreme delight the summer fait
Ye stupid countrey bumpkin such as ye John Barnarde.'

I cannot say whether or not the story is true, but even if it was concocted by Webbe, it illustrates that his sense of humour was at its height when he could laugh at somebody else's discomfort.

It seemed that quite frequently when I asked Webbe what he was doing, he would tell me that he was going into Cambridge, usually to 'trade' with somebody, as he put it. In fact it was merely further evidence that he was reliving repeatedly the final years of his life.

'What day is it?' I would ask him.

'Today is May 29th of ye year of Oure Lorde 1728. A pretty fine day I see but must to my glover Daniel Hardwicke in ye big towne of Cambridge. So out with ye horses and carriage and to ye towne at first time.'

'Who will you take with you?' I asked him.

'I fancey I go by myself since my goode wife is soon to beare childe by me and must reste. Shall take ye stupidde James Onyon my footman and servant.'

I began to wonder what his reaction would be if I were to ask if I could join him on his trip to Cambridge. When I asked if I could go with him, he had better ideas.

'It is now nighe on the eleventh houre and I shall leave within the houre of noone. I will too take you,' he agreed.

Then,

'Why do you not go in youre horseless carriage and take me with you. I shall join ye carte in the yarde and I may perchance to see you there,' he answered.

It became clear from an early stage of the Webbe writings that he had quite a strong sense of humour, although it was nearly always at the expense of someone else. He was the sort of man who would laugh at the village idiot placed in the stocks.

Robert Webbe, Gentleman, saw himself as having been endowed with a greater level of intelligence than the majority of the other village inhabitants, with the exception, of course, of other men equal or of higher standing within the village hierarchy, and interestingly, any tradesman on whom he relied for any kind of goods. Anybody who was below him on the social scale was somebody upon whom he looked down, his argument being that they must be stupid if they were not gentlemen. A 'stupid countrey bumpkin' is a term of ridicule that Webbe has used on several occasions to describe both myself and my father, and he invariably used it when referring to a person who did not share the same views as himself.

Webbe imagined that everyone should show a certain sense of politeness and deference to him, simply because he was permitted to use the title of 'Gentleman' after his name. He also liked to believe that he was a popular and well-liked member of the community. His writings often show him to have been a man who was bombastic and rough, with little sympathy for anybody, yet self-pitying—a person who would make fun of a hunchback. His depth of thinking, the spectrum of his ideas, and his philosophy were narrow—far narrower than he liked others to think. I suppose that really he was a typical eighteenth-century village squire, of whom there were a great number at that time.

Once I decided to ask Robert Webbe if he bore a coat-of-arms, because all gentlemen had one in that period. It was perhaps hard to imagine that he would admit to *not* having a coat-of-arms and, of course, he claimed that he had. Maybe he wanted to impress us with his answer to my question.

'Indeed I did as was such upon ye doors of my horse and carriage,' he wrote.

I requested him to illustrate for me his coat-of-arms and almost immediately he attempted to draw it for me. It was not easy to see what he was supposed to have depicted so I also asked him to describe it in writing for me. As if recognizing that his artistic talents were virtually non-existent, he continued,

'I do not fancy me as a painter but 'tis three shells two sheaves a river of Lynton with sheaves and ye family scorpionne.'

It seemed logical to us that his coat-of-arms, if it had really ever existed, should be made up of sheaves, if he was a 'trader of corn', and of the river which flowed through Linton.

I remember asking Webbe one day to write down for me the funniest story he could recollect—something though, which he had experienced. His story corroborated my thoughts that he would laugh at a hunchback. He told a story, which he found highly amusing, about a character called John Barnarde, a person to whom he had frequently referred. Barnarde was always described in derogatory terms by Webbe, and I suspect that he was regarded as the 'village idiot'. Maybe he was a mentally retarded or epileptic yokel.

The very idea of taking an eighteenth-century ghost to town in a car was a fantasy indeed! Then we began to wonder again if perhaps we were all affected by some kind of time-insanity.

Would normal rational people be thinking like this? We were not particularly concerned about what anybody else thought—anyway why should anybody else know? Probably if we had not regarded Robert Webbe as a person, or lodger in the house, we would have been intimidated and driven out of the house long before this.

Amidst much laughter, we got the car from the garage and parked it it the drive with all its doors open, although we could hardly imagine a portly Robert Webbe getting into it with his frock coat and breeches!

'We will take you to Cambridge in our horseless carriage at noon,' I told him.

'This is moste kinde of you and I am sorely tempted to take your ride. I shall come to see your carriage at noon or thereabouts and look well at it. If it tickles mine fancy to try this nonsense I shall order a ride around ye town here of Lynton. So to see you and ye horseless carriage at noone.'

I felt that I should ask him what he intended to buy in Cambridge.

'I shall buy for me a fine pair of kid gloves for ye *hand*some price of five shillings and some snuff for mine delicate nose. Also to see mine man Oliver Camperon in ye towne who desires to purchase some graine from me. Then to ye markett to see the goodes that catch mine pretty eyes.'

It seemed that Webbe was in a flippant mood and was not really taking my offer seriously. He was also trying to be funny—maybe it was merely an eighteenth-century sense of humour—with his reference to the gloves being a handsome price. Webbe underlined the first four letters in the word handsome.

Either we were unable to see Webbe if ever he went near the car, or he never left the house. Maybe he was only recalling what had happened to him on May 29th, 1728, while he was physically alive.

The latter idea seemed the most likely explanation. Curiously enough, however, this time the actual date, as far as we were concerned, was not May 29th. On previous occasions Webbe would write that the date where he was, was the same as the date on which I was receiving his automatic writing. On this particular occasion the date was June 8th, 1973.

Webbe's time scale appeared to move at a faster rate than our own. I had early on noticed that fact because whenever he was asked what the year was, he would always give a year between 1727 and 1733. As the writings with Webbe covered only a period of about seven years, it seemed obvious that his time was moving much faster than our own.

The final years of his life must have been rushing past him in a diminishing helter-skelter spiral. No wonder that he often seemed so confused.

Later that day, when we had garaged the car again, without having used it, I wrote at the top of a piece of paper,

'Did you pass any horseless carriages on your way to Cambridge?'

'I fancey I did take the quiet country road,' he replied, getting himself out of that trap.

'Did you buy your gloves?' I asked, assuming that he had returned from Cambridge. Webbe seemed to believe that he was still in Cambridge.

'Still in Cambridge am I and not yett have I purchased mine gloves. Must too see mine Mr Camperon for his graine. Soon I shall to buy mine gloves from ye shoppe of Hardwicke.'

'Why did you not come for a ride in our horseless carriage?'

'I did indeede see this fine carriage,' he claimed. 'A fearsome cart I see but seeing it still and with no horses I left in mine owne carriage. Your horseless carriage cannot and would not move for me.'

It seemed that if Webbe had seen this 'fine carriage' it was undoubtedly the shiny colour which would have attracted him to it. He must have been frightened by it if he had never seen anything like it before.

The theme of Webbe reliving scenes of his past life was gradually becoming stronger and stronger, and at times it was almost possible to feel his unspoken despair about his plight. He was being made to experience again and again different episodes from his life, not all of which were happy.

It was as if in death he had been shipwrecked while crossing the River Styx, and was now marooned on an island in the middle, watching everybody pass him by. No matter how hard he tried he could not make anybody notice him, and he had nothing on which he could float away from the island.

He had made one or two passing references to his son in previous automatic messages, but it was not until the scripts that I began to receive from him towards the end of 1972 that he expressed any concern over the health of John Webbe. He only seemed to show anxiety over the well-being of this one particular son—the others were rarely mentioned—which made me think that maybe John was not a healthy child by nature. Certainly as, according to Robert Webbe, he died young, this would make sense.

The first message in which he was mentioned came on another occasion when I had asked Robert Webbe what the date was.

'Why today [?] is in December. And so of too myne man Robert Moore for myne good foodes as my festive season approaches. And all myne children here to. Poor John likes ye snowe to much and poor fool will catch chill. But never does he lysten to his father.'

Obviously Webbe was experiencing a hard winter because he wrote after this,

'And just yesterday did I take a naughtye tumble in ye Market. Robert Webbe Gent: was the midle of much mockery and taunting. My poor behind did take the blow of myne tumble. And off to Harvey for a lotion. Such a blow to myne pride. But anon.'

The latter anecdote, although amusing, served to substantiate my theory that Robert Webbe was experiencing different episodes from the final years before his death. I really cannot conceive that he was still walking around the village as he saw it whilst he was alive, nor do I think these events which he was recounting were 'happening' in 1972.

The cause of John Webbe's death is not clear, but about three months after that message came another reference to his ill-health, and also to Robert Webbe's own illness.

'This day are my legs moste bad and wretched. I feel as of a tormented devill locked in hell. Still no sign of betterness from mine son John who I feare is soon to die, for so the bell tolls twelve. So is mine minde moste vexed. Must away too myne business and mine midday meale.'

John's death apparently occurred about three months later, which on our time scale was June 2nd, 1972. It was one of the few occasions when I felt compelled to sit down and communicate with Webbe. Usually I would be the instigator of the automatic writing; on this occasion I believe that it was his desire to tell me something.

John Webbe must have been an epileptic. After that Robert Webbe hardly ever mentioned John again, except on an occasion ten days later when it almost seemed that he had forgotten what he had already told me.

'... Poore son John did joyne ye service of God in ye last weeke. Ye poore childe did so die in painne, I fancey God's fine mercy did shine down on ye poore wretch.'

To begin with the fact that Robert Webbe should refer to his own recently deceased son as a 'poor wretch', rather surprised me. After thinking about it though, it did not strike me as quite so odd. I came to the conclusion that death was always within striking distance in the eighteenth century, more than it is now, and that people became far more reconciled to its reality.

Almost as if to reinforce my thoughts, a strange 'roll-call' appeared in automatic writing one morning in June, 1972, of persons who had apparently all died in Queen's House at various times. I had originally decided to put a question to Robert Webbe, but before he had an opportunity to reply, somebody else wrote instead.

'Susan Webb died on June 15th 1699 in this house aged fourteen years.

'Jo. Webb died also in 1597. Pray ye for his soul.

'Rob. Webbe did die here in this same house in ye yeare of 1733. May God rest his spirit.

'Also Elizabeth Webbe who died in 1737 in ye same house.

'Martha Webbe died too here in this place in 1747.

'Thos. Webbe died in his house in 1638. May God rest his poor soul.

'Richard Webbe too died in this house in ye yeare 1727. Rest my soul, Lord Jesus.'

At this point the end of the paper was reached and by the time I had found another sheet, I could get nothing. I do not know whether or not these people did in fact die in the house as they claimed to have done, but the 'message' was interesting in as much as each 'entry' was in a different handwriting.

After the death of his son John, Robert Webbe became increasingly preoccupied with his own illness and he would not hesitate to make mention of it at every available opportunity.

As if the outlet he had in my automatic writing was not enough, he also produced another rather unpleasant means of bringing attention to his obviously increasingly debilitating illness.

I think it was during this period that we discussed whether it might not be better to have his spirit exorcized.

# Five:      Three in a bed

It would invariably occur between midnight and two o'clock in the morning. It always happened in the same place, and it always happened to my father.

Until this point in 1972, I was really the only person to have 'experienced' Robert Webbe; others had noticed peculiar smells which we came to associate with him, and they had also been involved in other strange incidents, such as the lighting of our candles, and the writing of automatic scripts signed by Robert Webbe. Nobody else though had ever seen Webbe, or experienced him closely.

My parents' bedroom is at the front of the house and it is undoubtedly the room which would always have been occupied by the master of the house. It is believed that the bed has always been placed in the same position in the room, for the simple reason that there is no other practical position for it.

My father always sleeps on the right hand side of the bed, nearer to the main door which leads onto the landing. I think that probably the master of the house has always slept on this side of the bed simply because he would then be sleeping next to the main bedroom door.

From the onset of all the Webbe phenomena, the bed in this room was a focal point of attention for Webbe. I think this was probably due to the fact that the last conscious days or weeks of his life were in bed in this room, and probably he slept on the same side of the bed as my father. The covers on the bed would be found pulled back, the sheets all rumpled, and the pillows depressed as if somebody had been lying in the bed.

Then my father began to notice that 'somebody' had apparently been tampering with his pyjamas, which during the day he kept underneath his pillow in the made-up bed. The pyjamas were the usual trousers and shirt type of suit which buttoned up down the front. In order to remove the pyjamas, the buttons had to be unfastened; with the buttons undone, he would place the pyjamas under the pillow and make the bed.

Then he began to notice that when he went to bed at night, the buttons on the pyjamas would be fastened again. This happened maybe half a dozen times, although on the occasions when this occurred, the bed was always intact. If the bed had been disturbed, the pyjamas would be left alone.

As if this did not gain enough attention from any of us, another more bizarre phenomenon started to occur and it was interesting that once this new phenomenon commenced, the bed and the pyjamas were never disturbed again.

My father has described how he would be sleeping soundly when suddenly he would wake up for no obvious reason. But instead of being sleepy and only semi-conscious as one might expect when waking in the middle of the night, he was completely awake and very aware of everything in the room.

Often for a number of minutes nothing happened and he would begin to wonder why he had woken up, or rather *been* woken up.

He then underwent an experience as of somebody, whom he could not see, trying to climb into the bed at his side, but thwarted by the fact that my father was already in the bed.

Then, when whoever was trying to get into the bed had succeeded, my father received the distinct impression that somebody was actually lying in bed, but between himself and my mother who never woke up during one of these incidents. She always seemed to sleep through it, quite unaware of what was happening right next to her.

A little time later my father heard somebody breathing heavily into his right ear (this was not my mother's side of the bed) and this was accompanied by a smell of offensive halitosis which passed over his face, intermingled with a strong smell of tobacco. At the same time the sound of a man's stubbled chin rubbing against the sheets could be heard quite clearly. Despite the fact that on occasions my father held his breath and lay completely motionless, the breathing and the rubbing stubble sounds persisted, as did the fetor of halitosis. This, however, seemed to be merely the first phase of a longer experience.

While these sensations were occurring a new and different cycle of events began. My father described how a tingling sensation started in his toes. Gradually this spread to both of his feet, as though he had 'pins and needles'.

After some minutes the tingling spread up through the lower parts of his legs until a point was reached where the whole of the lower half of his body was tingling.

Then came the distinct experience that either somebody was lying on top of him, or he was lying *inside* somebody who had climbed into the bed. This was usually accompanied by an overbearing feeling of oppression.

And then, as suddenly as it started, it would abruptly cease, and he would find himself alert in bed with nothing odd happening.

My father has always been rather disinclined to talk about these experiences, although I am not sure why. He had experienced these sensations three or four times when I decided to try an experiment.

I decided to ask 'Thomas Penn', the now-famous doctor who, given the birth date of the person concerned, produces medical diagnoses in automatic writing through my hand, to diagnose Robert Webbe's illness. I was interested to find out from what he had died, although obviously it was a disease connected with his legs—that was reasonably obvious because he was always referring to his 'troublesome legs', and on the occasion when I had seen his apparition he had been supporting himself on a pair of sticks. The only obstacle was that I did not know Webbe's birth date. Rather than disturb Webbe any further at a time when I felt it would be better to ignore him because of the trouble he was causing the family, I asked Thomas Penn to try to make a diagnosis of Robert Webbe, whom I thought had probably died in 1733.

After waiting a couple of minutes, I began to write automatically in the hand writing of Thomas Penn.

'I think you will find that Mr Webbe died of *gout*.

'This is a painful disease in which there is an excess of uric acid in the blood. Heredity may have been important. Alcohol plays a great part in the causation of gout and the fermented liquors are more dangerous than distilled spirits. Rich food in excess combined with a lack of exercise and indulgence in liquor may mean suffering for the patient. A combination of poor food and faulty hygiene combined with malted liquor causes a "poor man's gout".

'An acute attack of gout, as I believe Mr Webbe suffered, begins with warning twinges of pain in the joints of the hands and feet and the patient becomes restless and irritable. In the small hours of the morning he may be awakened by a severe pain in the big toe, usually on the right side, which rapidly becomes swollen, red and shiny and agonisingly painful. The temperature rises. The pain subsides somewhat during the day but returns at night. There may be three or four such attacks during the year. Hard stone-like deposits in the cartilage of the ear or around the knuckles are characteristic of gout. He should have lived a temperate life eating moderately of a diet restricted in meat and starches. Alcohol must be avoided and salt should be left out of food.'

The picture was beginning to clear. Nearly everything which Thomas Penn had described here would fit Webbe, and it was surprising how many of the symptoms of gout my father had suffered during the bed experience, and yet he did not himself actually suffer from gout.

Thomas Penn could almost have been describing what my father had felt—the twinge of pain in the hands and feet, the waking in the small hours of the morning, even the fact that there were usually three or four such attacks during the course of a year.

Robert Webbe must have nurtured, unsuspectingly, the ideal conditions for fostering an attack of gout. He had made reference on numerous occasions to eating and drinking, and probably most eighteenth-century liquors were fermented, and I cannot remember him ever having made a reference to exercise. Obviously the levels of hygiene were not as high as they are now; the mention that salt be omitted from the diet of a patient with gout is also interesting since salting was the chief method of preserving foodstuffs until refrigeration.

Robert Webbe, I decided, almost certainly died from gout.

After my father had undergone this experience three times, it did not occur again until the same time the following year, in 1973. It was not, however, until the third series of 'attacks' in 1974 that we talked about doing something to prevent it—what we were not sure.

The only reason that we considered taking action at so late a time was because the experience seemed to be becoming more intense, almost as if my father was being absorbed by this spirit, whose main motive, we thought, was domination.

The following is a transcript of an account that my father wrote, describing what was to be the last time this unpleasant experience occurred. It is dated Tuesday, December 17th, 1974.

'Matthew went to bed early at 9.30 p.m. but my wife and I went to bed at about 11.20 p.m. From the sound of regular breathing, I was aware that my wife quickly went to sleep. I, however, was unable to go to sleep and lay on my right side with the bedclothes above my left ear and my eyes closed. I was quite still.

'Some time later at about 11.40 p.m., although my eyes were still closed, I was aware of being able to see a colour, a beautiful violet-purple. It was sometimes brighter in the centre and sometimes brighter around the circumference. I also had the feeling that I was standing in a cave, looking out onto a purple sky, with rocks all around the entrance of the cave.

'Another analogy that occurred to me was that my eye was in the centre of someone's open mouth and that I was looking out through their teeth. The purple colour was not static; in fact there was considerable movement like clouds passing over the sun which varied its intensity.

'This experience persisted for some minutes. Then I heard the characteristic stubble prickle on my left cheek. It sounded quite loud, clear and unmistakable and preceded the "arrival" of Webbe's entity where I lay. I was unable to produce this sound myself. I remained impressed by the beauty of the earlier colour and tried to will that it should be green not purple, but I was not successful with this. However, the purple colour returned less enduringly and there was then the sensation that my body was being alternately stretched and compressed. A third colour sensation subsequently occurred, followed by a feeling that a large hand was being rubbed over me, above the bedclothes. A fourth colour sensation took place, this time accompanied by a prickling sensation in my lower right leg.

'Throughout this time I had lain motionless with my eyes closed. I now cautiously opened one eye and then the other. I was surprised that I still had the ability to see in the lower half of my vision the persistent purple colour. Again there was a tingling sensation in the entire lower half of my body; I think that there were two further sensations during which the tingling became more widespread and occupied my whole body.

'I then mentally said,

' "Go away. I have had enough. I must have sleep."

'I repeated this several times and I felt a certain sense of upheaval, as though a "departure" was actually occurring. I continued with my mental instructions in a more aggressive, bullying form and I was surprised at the apparent relationship between my instructions and the tingling sensations. I said silently,

' "Go away. I shall tell Matthew," and repeated it several times.

'Again there was widespread tingling. After a short while I repeated the name Matthew four times with no other words and was surprised at the tingling response obtained. I again opened my eyes and could see not only the characteristic purple but also a yellowy-topaz colour. I had the impression that both colours were waning. My wife jolted in bed and I wondered whether the sensations had transferred to her and whether she had been awakened.

' "Are you awake?" I whispered twice.

'I got no answer.

'Gradually the experience dwindled and some time later I fell asleep. I estimate the duration of the entire occurrence as probably half an hour.'

This experience, although it was the last one of such an intensity, was interesting because it was the only time my father had actually been awake when it had begun. He has never actually seen Webbe during these experiences, although he remains sure, as does everybody else, that it was caused by Robert Webbe.

Undoubtedly these experiences are a reflection of what Webbe suffered during the final years of his life whilst dying from gout. He was reliving those experiences in the same place as they had occurred whilst he was alive, and it was merely coincidental that my father happened to be in the same place at the time. The experience was therefore transferred directly to him. If anybody happened to lie in that position in the bed where Webbe probably died, I expect that they too might experience similar sensations.

It was at this time that the Vicar of Linton, the Rev. David Walser, who was acquainted with the house and our experiences with Robert Webbe, offered to say prayers for him in the hope that he would find some level of peace. By now it was quite clear that Webbe was trapped in the house, reliving his past life.

We decided to wait and see what happened—if things got worse we thought we should do something. I was not certain in any case that saying prayers in the house would be of great benefit because I was not sure that it was necessarily what Robert Webbe wanted. He had never made any mention of wishing that he could leave the house—he always seemed fascinated by what was going on and who was living in his house. He had not wanted to leave his house behind and so he had stayed with it, although on occasions he had seemed perplexed that there were strangers in it with whom he was not acquainted, and who displeased him by their disregard of his presence.

Bearne

1717

(42)

1.8.71

E^d Benj: Cd.* 73

Oliver Cromwell

1643

(59)

1.8.71

## Three in a bed

It was as though he had overheard our discussion about help-
ing him to leave, because he now became quieter, as though
reluctant to upset us in case we sent him away. In this, he
seemed almost child-like.

The bed experience was not repeated again except on two
occasions, the second of which was particularly interesting.

I had travelled to Japan in July, 1976, to participate in a
television programme which had started at 7.30 p.m. (Japanese
local time) and which lasted until 9.00 p.m.

A part of the programme was devoted to the apport phenomenon connected with Robert Webbe. A film of the interior
of Queen's House was also shown on the programme, although
only the apports were discussed.

We discussed Robert Webbe between 7.45 p.m. and 8.00 p.m.

Meanwhile, back in England, my father was experiencing
Robert Webbe trying to get into his side of the bed again—the
first time it had happened for nearly eighteen months. There
ensued the usual tingling sensations and the sounds he had come
to associate with Webbe, and he estimated that this particular
experience lasted for approximately fifteen minutes and
occurred at about four o'clock in the morning.

The time difference between Britain and Japan during the
summer time is eight hours, Tokyo being eight hours ahead of
London. My father had his experience with Webbe, the first
for many months, only about twelve hours after I had been discussing him on the other side of the world.

It seemed that it did not matter where I discussed Robert
Webbe, because he still caused effects in Queen's House.

When the bed experiences were first noticed, in 1972, another
phenomenon commenced around Easter of that year, which
baffled the family on the few occasions that it happened, probably because we did not immediately associate it with Robert
Webbe.

It began at lunch when the whole family were at home, eating
in the dining room. We were not even talking about Webbe,
which perhaps is why we did not associate what happened with
him.

There was suddenly a loud slamming sound which we all heard. It was as though somebody had gone out of the front door, leaving it to swing shut behind them.

My mother got up, went into the hallway, and found that the front door was not properly closed. She shut it and locked it again. We all assumed that somebody in the family had been out of the door before luncheon and had omitted to close it properly, so that the wind had caught it and caused it to slam. We thought no more of it.

The following day whilst we were again having lunch in the dining room, the front door was heard to slam shut again.

'I wish people would make sure that they shut that door properly when they go out of it,' said my mother, and again it was closed securely and locked.

It still did not strike anybody as odd.

When the same thing happened on the third consecutive day at about the same time, and under the same circumstances, our suspicions were aroused. Again the door was found unlocked and swinging. Nobody had been out of the door that morning. But we thought of the incident as just another of those odd and inexplicable events which happen occasionally.

The next day at lunch time we all sat and waited for the door to slam so that we could all rush out to see who was there— or not there!

The door did not slam. Neither did it do so the following lunch time, probably because we were again expecting it to do so.

Two days later it occurred again and nobody was to be seen. This time we knew that it had been locked because my parents had been keeping an observant eye on it, to ensure that it remained locked.

It was now that we began to suspect Robert Webbe of leaving the house through the front door, allowing it to slam behind him. If he could produce strange objects in the house, and write on the walls, why should he not use the front door. The door had been there during his lifetime, so there was logic that if he still occupied the house, he should use it.

The next day Thursday, April 20th, we devised an experiment to identify whoever was using the front door and allowing it to slam shut during lunch.

We covered the hall floor with sheets of newspaper over which we spread a thick layer of dampened sand so as to prevent it being disturbed by draughts. The intention was to record the footprints of whoever walked through the hall. It was now impossible to reach the front door without walking across the sand.

Ensuring that the door was securely fastened, and that the sand was undisturbed we sat down in the dining room and started our luncheon.

Even though this time we were again listening and waiting (which previously seemed to have been an inhibiting factor) the door did suddenly crash shut. We had not heard anybody walk through the hallway.

When we reached the sand we were startled to find a pair of footprints in it, and a small hole in the sand on either side of each footprint.

It is difficult to say just why we were startled to find the sand disturbed; after all, we had placed it there for that very purpose. I think we did not really expect to record anything.

The footprints brought Robert Webbe closer to us, in that they made us feel that he was more human—not merely a phantom who inhabited our house and caused ghostly things to happen. Traditionally ghosts were white sheet-like figures who glided around leaving no trace of themselves. Robert Webbe was different.

We were not very sure what to do with these footprints now that we had recorded them in the sand. From our first inspection, they did not seem to resemble even remotely any footprints that might be made by anybody in the house. They were far too small, and from what we could see without disturbing the sand too much, they did not resemble the shape of the sole of any modern shoe.

We obtained some plaster of Paris and decided to make a plaster cast of the foot marks. It was easier to make separate casts rather than try to make one large one, so I placed a cardboard 'fence' around the first imprint and poured plaster into it. After it had set we found that the sand had been too dry and had collapsed under the weight of the plaster, effectively destroying one of the two prints.

After spraying the remaining one lightly with water I succeeded in producing a sharp cast of the footprint; I then cleared away the sand.

Maybe the plaster cast had some magic quality which took away Webbe's energy, but the front door never slammed again.

We checked the cast against every shoe in the house and it matched none. Not only was the actual shape of the sole considerably different, but the size was very much smaller, especially in length, than any modern shoes. The cast seemed to be of a shoe with a high heel, and was only eight inches long, from the tip of the toe to the back of the heel. Most of the shoes that we possessed were at least ten inches in length.

Could it have been Webbe's intention to demonstrate that he was as physical as ourselves, or was it because he thought that we were not convinced by the evidence we had already, that Webbe decided that he would have to try even harder to convince us of his presence?

# Six:     'I go and I come'

I began to form the impression that Robert Webbe became more active if I communicated with him in automatic writing. If I did not converse with him, we noticed no side effects such as the disturbed bed, the untraceable odours, or the apports. My automatic writing seemed to motivate him into action.

At one time, in 1973, when we felt that Webbe was becoming too overbearing I did not communicate with him for a number of months, and we soon noticed a difference in the levels of 'interference'. This method of keeping him quiet could only be maintained for a few months though. After that, he seemed to be able to muster up enough energy to produce phenomena, albeit weak, more or less of his own accord, but certainly with little provocation from myself. We soon realized that we only had to discuss him, and later merely to think about him, for strange audible phenomena to occur.

For example, we might be seated in the dining room, when everyone would hear the sound of footsteps walking across the empty room above. There was little point in rushing upstairs to see who was there—we knew we were the only people in the house.

Things then became rather more odd, and we began to wonder whether some of us were imagining things, or whether others of us were deaf. Often we might be together in the same room, usually the dining room as the family tended to congregate there, when three members of the family would insist that they distinctly heard somebody on the stairs, while the other two would say that they heard nothing.

I know that I have heard footsteps when others have been adamant that they heard nothing; then I wonder how they could possibly not have heard what I heard. On occasions, others claimed to have heard heavy footsteps while I remained unaware of them.

Most of the sounds that we heard were of footsteps, usually in the room above the dining room, which at that time was an empty bedroom, or on the staircase. I shall never forget one particular Sunday morning when I was in the kitchen discussing Robert Webbe with my mother, who was preparing lunch.

The rest of the family was outside in the garden when suddenly we both heard a terrible sound, extremely loud and clear, as though somebody was being throttled or choked, originating, we thought, from the front of the house.

We were both so startled that we rushed into the study, from where we guessed the noise had emanated, only to find the room quite empty.

'That comes of talking about Webbe,' I said, although still puzzled.

If it was Webbe, I cannot think why he should have made such a grotesque sound.

On another occasion, again a Sunday, we were sitting in the dining room having tea, when each of us quite distinctly heard the sound of a large coin being dropped on the floor in the hall. It sounded as though it had been dropped from the staircase onto the stone floor below, and it seemed to roll around in circles before coming to rest. Again, although we knew there was nobody in the house, we still rushed into the hall to look for the coin. Of course, when I asked him about it, Webbe claimed to have dropped a coin on the staircase.

It was clear that he would accept responsibility for almost anything we cared to blame on him.

Another thing we heard very frequently was the ringing of what sounded like a small handbell. This we first noticed in the summer of 1976, and it seemed to coincide with the period during which I was planning this book. What was interesting about the handbell was that it would always occur at the same time in the evening, at about 6.35, almost as if it was summoning Webbe to dinner; we invariably heard it shortly after we all sat down to eat. It would usually be heard by only three out of the five people present, although those three people seemed to be chosen to hear it in rotation!

Finally, on the day when I began to write the first draft of the book, I was tormented by this tinkling bell. I counted it ringing on at least fifteen occasions during that day. The following day I worked outside in the garden, and was undisturbed.

When I was eventually compelled by the weather to continue my writing in the house, I was once more forced to leave the room in which I was working, this time by an overpowering smell of sewage. Even when all the windows were open I was unable to dispel the odour, although I noticed that it was confined to the room in which I was working. My brother, who was in the house at the time, could also smell it strongly. I finally overcame the problem by spraying the room heavily with an aerosol air freshener.

In previous years we had made some interesting tape recordings simply by leaving a tape recorder running in a room, usually the study, with the microphone plugged in but the volume turned right down so that theoretically it was impossible to record anything. This is actually the standard method of producing what is known as the electronic voice phenomenon, discovered by Friedrich Jurgenson, and pioneered by Dr Konstantin Raudive.

I was aware of Jurgenson's discovery, and his work, as I had earlier met him and participated in some informal experiments with him. In 1959, Jurgenson had discovered that if he left a tape recorder running in the manner that I have just described, it would pick up strange sounds and voices which he had not heard at the time his machine was recording. Subsequently many scientists were able to repeat his experiments and obtain similar results but without satisfactory explanation.

During the first occasion on which I tried experimenting with a small cassette player owned by my sister, I left it running in the study for a few minutes.

I rewound the tape and, turning the volume up, listened. At first there was a lot of static noise, as one would expect.

I am not sure what I *was* expecting.

After about fifteen seconds a church bell could be heard quite clearly tolling. The bell tolled slowly six times and the rest of the tape was filled with the usual hissing of unrelieved silence. I had not heard bells ringing when I made the recording, yet it sounded almost as if I had recorded them while standing next to the church in which they were tolling. My parents, who heard my recording, also knew that there had been no bells ringing.

I tried to repeat my first results several more times that evening but was unsuccessful.

Even stranger than the recording of the bell on the tape was the fact that the next morning when we went to play it, the bell was no longer to be heard. I am sure that I did not erase the recording, either deliberately or accidentally. This was unusual to say the least, and Jurgenson's recordings were not in the habit of disappearing. If the sound could find its way onto the tape in the first place, when it should have been impossible, why could it not remove itself again?

On subsequent occasions I was able to repeat my success, although not always with such good results. I soon discovered that the best recordings were to be obtained in the front of the house, especially in the room we used as a study. Of course, this was the part of the house which had been built by Robert Webbe.

When we began to consider the sounds, we realized that all the phenomena connected with Robert Webbe were associated with the areas of the house which he had built, with the exception of the footsteps that we occasionally heard above the dining room.

When the tape recorder was placed in my parents' bedroom a range of sounds, from heavy footsteps across the room to a hammering sound which seemed to originate from the direction of the panelling, could be heard. Occasionally one could hear muffled talking, which was incomprehensible, except that one could tell that it was a man's voice.

The most fascinating recordings, however, were made in the room which we used as our study, but which Webbe claimed to have used as his dining room.

Here the recordings would usually begin with the banging of a large gong (there has never been a gong in the house while we have lived in it). Later Webbe told me that he knew when his dinner was ready because his maid Betsy would bang a gong. This would be followed by silence for usually twenty or thirty seconds, after which the sound of crockery being moved about was audible. It sounded as though plates were being laid on a table.

Speech was rarely heard, but if it was it was usually muffled and unintelligible. The recordings usually sounded as though they were being made from outside the room, so that everything was recorded at a distance, and it was not easy to make sense of the scene inside the room, or the conversation, without actually seeing what was happening. Perhaps, it later occurred to me, families ate in silence during the eighteenth century.

The recordings would regularly be punctuated by belches, presumably from Robert Webbe. There would also be profuse grunting sounds, usually following what we guessed was a coin falling onto the bare wooden floor. (The floor in this room has always been covered while we have lived in the house.)

Another interesting recording that I made in the study by the same method was of a piece of music played on an organ. But instead of the organ being electric, it was a pipe organ. It sounded to us like a piece of eighteenth-century funeral music. It was so clear on the tape that it could have been recorded inside a church.

However, the tape recordings met a sad end one day when my sister, who owned both the tapes and the recorder, decided that what I had recorded frightened her. She wiped the tape clean without consulting anybody. In any case, my impecunious sister decided to sell the machine, thus putting an end once and for all to my experiments.

By this time it was also becoming apparent that Webbe's activities were 'peaking' in cycles of approximately six months. We noticed that we had many more incidents which we could attribute to him during August and December each year, although we could not explain this. This was particularly obvious with the apport phenomenon—nearly all the apports arrived during one of those two months.

I think that our reaction to Webbe and the various phenomena associated with him is interesting. Although from a long-term point of view we were not particularly worried or frightened by him and, as I have said, we treated him more as a lodger, we were often startled or scared momentarily by him. I think that was due mainly to the sheer unexpectedness of what happened. Something always occurred when we were least expecting it, and this invariably caught us unawares. No one went up the stairs searching for strange materializations, nobody ever sat waiting for odd noises or sounds to come through the air; these things would always happen as we went about our daily lives, with the occasional exception of sounds which would be heard if we had discussed Webbe for any length of time. He always made us jump.

I remember one night I was passing through the hall to the front of the house when I noticed the strongest smell of tobacco smoke I had ever smelled in the house. It was so strong that I thought somebody had walked through smoking a pipe. I quickly realized that it was the smell which indicated that Webbe was passing through, and I was curious to follow the trail he had left behind.

It quickly led me away from the hallway and up to the top of the stairs onto the landing. All the lights were switched on so the area was well lit.

I now thought that the smell was becoming even stronger; I walked quickly across the landing and into my sister's bedroom. She was in bed, but awake. My parents were downstairs at the other end of the house and out of earshot.

'Can you smell anything?' I asked her, noticing that the smell had not reached her room.

She could not.

By now the tobacco smell had spread along the landing and had reached the closed door of my parents' bedroom. I thought that it was stronger now than it had been at the bottom of the

*Thomas Burman*

1722

Edm Edmoonds
1694
(16)
31·7·71

*Philip Sadler 1773*

Charles *Ashby 191*

I. G
1727

John Burroughs
1773
(73) 1·8·71

(30) 31·7·71

Samuel Swale
1620

321

*Swale 1707*

P. Rogers
1759
(82)

stairs, but I was not sure that I was not just imagining that it was intensifying.

I pushed open the door of my parents' room to find out if the smell was in there also. The curtains were drawn and the room was in darkness, but as I opened the door, it was filled with the light which swept in from the landing.

I took a few steps into the room and sniffed. I was quite sure now that the smell was stronger than it had been downstairs. I quickly cast a glance around to check that nobody was there and stood by the door inhaling the smoky aroma in the dusky air.

Suddenly my eyes were riveted to a spot on the floor near a cupboard on the opposite side of the room. How on earth had he got there, I asked myself? A moment before I had looked at that spot and noticed nothing. There, within a few feet of me, was the figure of Robert Webbe.

It was he; there was no doubt in my mind that it was the same 'person' I had seen standing on the staircase one winter evening the previous year. I stood transfixed, like a rabbit temporarily dazzled by the headlamps of an approaching car. I was unable to speak—but then what would I have said?

I twisted my body round so that I could reach the light switch, all the time trying not to let him out of my sight for a fraction of a second. I did not relish the thought of being in a badly lit room with him. I suddenly realized that I was extremely frightened but I could not understand why. Perhaps it was a flash-back to a childhood fear of meeting a ghost in a darkened room.

Switching on the bedroom lights, my uneasiness dissolved.

Webbe was still standing there, seemingly unaware that anything was happening, or even that I was in the room. He stood, supporting his short portly body on a pair of sticks which looked as though they had not long been cut from a hedge, staring vacantly towards me, but not at me. He seemed not to be moving, and for a moment I wondered if I was imagining his presence. I closed my eyes and could see nothing. He was still standing on the opposite side of the room when I opened my eyes again.

Webbe was as real as the furniture in the room. He looked so real that it seemed hard to imagine that he was no more than a ghost. He reminded me of a wax figure from Madam Tussaud's. I could not really imagine that he was able to come and go in thin air, while I was quite unable to see through him. He was not shadowy, or pale. He was, to all intents and purposes, a physical being.

Up to this point he had been standing statuesquely, like an effigy that had escaped from a museum. Then slowly his gaze moved from the area in which I was standing, to the bed. It was the fact that he had said nothing, or rather that I had heard nothing, which was particularly uncanny.

Without really being aware of what I was doing, I moved one step towards him. Simultaneously he moved one step back so that I was still the same distance from him. It was like trying to touch water in a mirage, I thought, as I tried to edge close enough to touch him. Now I seemed to have a heightened awareness of what I was doing, almost as if I was standing outside myself, watching Matthew Manning semi-mesmerized by this person. I sensed that it was rather unpleasant that I could be so easily 'controlled' by this figure. I could 'hear' the thoughts running through my head.

'Be careful. You don't know what might happen', I could hear myself saying.

'Well, there's not much he can do to you,' was my reply to myself.

From outside myself I could sense a strange conflict taking place between me and Webbe. I was aware that he was trying to draw something out from deep down inside me, but I did not know what this might be.

Then I watched myself get bolder. I took two steps forward with no hesitation, holding out my hand in front of me.

Yet all the time his eyes were fixed on that bed, almost as if he was staring at a body which he recognized lying there. For this move, he took two steps back.

'You'll corner him soon,' Matthew said, 'because he can only take one step back now before he reaches the wall.'

'And then he'll probably vanish into thin air,' I warned myself.

'I only want to shake hands with you,' said Matthew, offering his hand to Webbe.

His baleful eyes swivelled round towards me. This almost pitiful figure hardly matched the ebullient, effervescent and bombastic author of the automatic writings which he was supposed to have transmitted. This man looked tired and brimming with sadness.

As soon as I spoke, it was as though a warmth kindled suddenly inside the worn figure. I saw that his eyes seemed to brighten, and he quickly, although with some difficulty, grasped two sticks in one hand, leaving the other hand free. He held out his hand.

This was the person with whom I had been communicating. But it was not the empty shell of a person who had been standing in front of me a few seconds before—or at least I thought it was a few seconds before. Time really did not matter now. In fact nothing really seemed to matter. Everything seemed strangely transformed.

I noticed that the frilled cuff poking out from the sleeve of Webbe's coat was grubby.

The next moment something inexplicable happened, and I was aware that I was now no longer watching myself. I seemed to be one person instead of two.

At the same moment I saw that my hand was shaking the air.

Robert Webbe had not vanished—he was still standing in front of me, but my hand passed straight through his. He may still have looked physical but he was like a mirage.

Then for the first time he spoke, complaining of his 'blessed legs', and rapping a stick on the floor.

'Stay there for a moment,' I told him, 'I have something for you.' I was not sure for a moment whether I ought to call him, 'Sir'.

I made a dash for the door and ran into my sister's room.

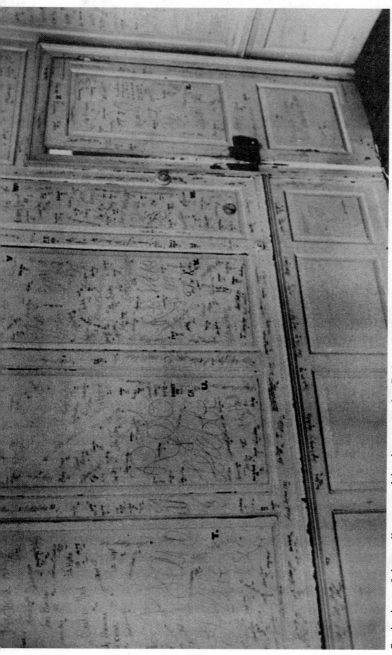

7. A view of the walls covered in signatures by Robert Webbe in 1971. 'Indeede I did see your owne fine workes on my familye and did decide to helpe you by allowing my frendes to sign their names on the wall.'

8. The collection of objects which appeared as apports in the house. Robert Webbe claimed they were gifts for us although their origin was never traced.

9. The loaf found on the staircase, with two cigarettes also left by Webbe.

'Quick, give me something I can give to Webbe. He's in there.'

I picked up a doll's wooden clog and asked if I could have it.

'Why don't you come and see him too?' I asked her.

'You must be joking,' she said, obviously now as frightened as I had been at first. I was not going to wait to persuade her at the risk of Webbe vanishing once more.

He was still there when I got back into the room, looking sorrowfully at the bed.

Suddenly I was watching Matthew again, standing in front of Webbe. Both seemed rather wary of each other, like a pair of fighters. Matthew gingerly approached Webbe, holding the clog in the palm of his outstretched hand, and said,

'Here is a present for you. You can keep it.'

I watched Webbe extending his fingers towards the clog lying on Matthew's hand and he quickly made a grab for it, as though catching a butterfly which had settled on a flower.

My hand was empty, and I realized once more that as soon as Webbe had made contact with my hand, I had stopped watching myself from the outside again.

He looked at the wooden clog he now held in his hand— the same hand that only a few moments ago I had been unable to grasp.

Then he put it into the pocket of his equally elusive coat, and I was unable to see it any more. He seemed to be growing impatient as he rapped his sticks on the floor. I was not sure if it was my imagination, but I thought that the room was becoming chilly.

As soon as the wooden clog had been placed into the pocket a most extraordinary thing began to happen.

It was as though I was watching a colour television screen from which the colour was gradually fading.

I noticed that the figure of Robert Webbe was losing its colour around the edges, so that his outer areas were greyish, while the main central areas of his body were still showing colour.

While I watched, I could see the colour vanishing as if it had been contained by a stopper which had now been removed. Within less than thirty seconds, I estimated, all the colour had gone and I was left facing a shadowy grey figure.

Then the grey became fainter, and I realized that he was vanishing—into the air.

I was standing in the empty bedroom, wondering if it was night time and if I had been sleep-walking, I still had my clothes on and my parents' bed was empty.

I knew that the wooden clog I had been holding had gone. He could not really have taken it, I thought. It was not on the floor where he had been standing, nor was it elsewhere in the room.

My sister, meanwhile, although she had been too frightened to venture into the bedroom with me, had been trying to hear what was going on from her own room. She claimed that the only words she heard spoken were my own—she had not heard anybody complaining about legs. She had, however, heard sharp raps coming from the room 'as though someone was banging on the radiator'.

What, I wondered, were my parents going to say? The experience had been real for me, and as long as I knew that it had really happened, I was not too concerned about what others might think or say.

I rushed downstairs to find them, and excitedly I told them what I had seen. Before I had finished talking they were half way up the stairs.

Webbe was not to be seen, but he had left his mark. The reek of tobacco smoke still pervaded the entire area of the staircase and landing.

My parents were fascinated, and had no reason to doubt me. After all, everybody in the house knew of Webbe's existence, and everybody could recall their own personal experiences.

I think that on that particular night, Webbe had walked from his dining room at the front of the house, up the staircase to his 'bedchamber'. I would never have seen him, had it not been for the fact that I could smell tobacco smoke and had followed its trail out of curiosity. I really do not know, if anybody else would have seen him had they been with me. I know that I am the only person ever to have *seen* him in this way.

I began to think over what had happened during those two or three minutes—the approximate duration of the experience I guessed. Why had I not had the curious battling feelings, and the feelings of being drawn out of my body to watch myself from outside, on the first occasion on which I had seen Webbe, on the staircase?

I never really found answers to satisfy myself. I know that on the second occasion I was in closer physical proximity, and I also noticed that I felt as though I had come back into my body on each occasion that I had 'touched', or made contact with, the area of empty space being occupied by Robert Webbe.

The more I thought about it, the more convinced I became that Webbe's 'spirit' was some kind of incandescent light. A bulb will only light up when connected to a source of electricity, like a battery, and I came to the conclusion that I was the battery for Robert Webbe. I could not help thinking of how he had looked wax-like and lifeless, until I had spoken to him. He had almost come back to life then.

For several months after this encounter, no phenomena that could be immediately associated with him occurred. I did not pursue the automatic writings and, in fact, retrospectively I now realize that this was the peak of the Webbe activity—it was never really the same after that. The 'physical' side of his manifestations grew weaker and weaker.

It was partly a natural running down I think on his part, and partly deliberate on my part, because I began to feel that Webbe was becoming too powerful a character in our lives.

# Seven:     'I am Millicent'

In the last chapter I recounted how footsteps had been heard coming from the bedroom above the dining room; at that time the bedroom was empty because it was in too bad a state of repair to use. During 1973, my parents made it more habitable—it had a new ceiling, the walls were papered, and the windows replaced, and towards the end of the year it was almost ready for me to occupy.

The footsteps really did not concern us, especially as the family had experienced far more unnerving things in the house. We always thought, however, that it was rather odd that they should come from that particular room because it was not in Robert Webbe's domain. Apart from anything else, we did not hear them regularly—maybe once a month or so.

On one occasion my brother, who was ill in bed in the adjacent bedroom, reported that he had heard quite clearly somebody walking about in my bedroom, although the house had been empty. At other times he said that he had heard somebody walk through the room while he had been in the bathroom and on going to see who was coming, had discovered no one.

Robert Webbe never mentioned this area of the house in his automatic writings: he was concerned only with what he considered to be 'his' section of the house.

One of the last things that had to be done to the room was the staining of the skirting boards, which was a task for my mother. She finally found time one evening when my father and I were out of the house and my brother had gone to bed.

It was a Sunday, in December, 1973; she had just gone into the washing cubicle adjoining my bedroom when she heard somebody walking heavily across the room, from one door to the other.

'Did you enjoy yourself?' she called out, not looking to see who had entered the room, but assuming that it was my father.

There was no answer, and glancing out from the washing cubicle she saw the room was empty. She continued with her job thinking he had not heard.

Fifteen minutes after she had called out, we did both come in. Then she discovered that neither of us had walked across the room—we had not even been in the house.

I was looking forward to moving into the room, it was much more comfortable than the study in which I had been sleeping previously. The room had a beautifully tranquil and undisturbed atmosphere and a warm glow of old oak—certainly there was nothing 'spooky' about it.

Obviously, as I was in unfamiliar surroundings, I had difficulty in getting to sleep that first night. The light came in through the windows in all sorts of places that were not the same as in the study and, because the room was not facing the High Street, it was considerably quieter. 'Tomorrow night will be better,' I told myself.

The next night, however, it was just the same. I could not sleep properly and spent most of the night restlessly awake. I was still sure that it was just a psychological reaction to an environmental change.

How long was it going to take me to get used to the room, I asked myself after a fifth consecutive disturbed night?

By now it was Christmas Eve, and we were all preparing to travel to my grandmother's house for Christmas.

Maybe because the house was about to become empty, or maybe for other reasons, Robert Webbe was that year conspicuous by his absence. There were no messages or stories about Christmas time, and no mysterious objects left lying on the stairs, although we returned home again on Boxing Day. Perhaps in his helter-skelter time cycle, it was not Christmas for him. Or perhaps he really had gone.

Despite the fact that while I had been away for Christmas, I had occupied a strange room, I had had no difficulty in sleeping there. But as soon as I spent a night in my own bedroom, I could not sleep properly again.

Gradually, I began to sleep more easily, but the only problem was that I seemed always to awaken in the middle of the night.

Then things began to change—I would still wake in the early hours of the morning, but now I would have an irrational impression that there was somebody standing next to my bed. I thought it was a young girl, but I could not say why I felt that; I just knew.

I sensed that she was not malicious, or malevolent. She seemed lost, or in need of help. But it was ridiculous—why should I be thinking this about something I could not see?

After two more nights spent with the same experience, I decided to find out what I could through automatic writing. It was not Robert Webbe this time, I was sure.

The next night I went to bed, leaving by my side and in easy reach, some paper and my fountain pen. If I was disturbed again, I would try some automatic writing; if I slept soundly, then obviously I would not bother.

I did not sleep well. At about two o'clock next morning, I woke up, or rather I felt as if I had been woken up, by somebody who had penetrated my sleep by whispering through my dreamy subconscious.

'Help me. Help me.'

Grabbing the paper and pen, I wrote at the top of the sheet, 'Who is in this room?'

'I am Millicent born here 1655,' immediately came the reply.

'Not another one,' I thought, 'Robert Webbe's enough.'

'What do you want,' I wrote brusquely, as if I had been called to the telephone in the middle of the night by someone to whom I did not wish to speak.

'Peace. Just peace,' she answered.

'How old are you', I asked becoming more interested.

'XV,' was all she wrote.

'When did you die,' I asked.

'1670 here.'

'Who were your parents.'

'Ruth and Henry Webbe,' came the reply.

So this was another Webbe, although, if she was to be believed, she died eight years before Robert Webbe was born.

I asked from what she died.

'My child. Birth and death. Ask not of who. I cannot say. It is not happy. My baby is gone.' The answer came in staccato breaks.

'How old are you?' I asked her again. She had written fifteen the first time, but I wanted to check.

'XV,' she repeated.

'What do you want me to do for you?'

'My childe. Pray to God. I am lost. Look at the chylde. I must hurry to kill it. Forgive me my sins. I cannot forever suffer. Please for me,' and it tailed off into nothingness, before she signed.

'Millicent Webbe MDCLXX.'

She had, it seemed, given birth to an illegitimate child, whose father was either unknown, or else she did not wish to disclose his name. She had killed the child at birth, probably because of the social circumstances of the times. It would seem that she had died at about the same time.

There did not seem much that I could do, so I did not pursue the matter further that night, although I slept soundly.

I was interested to find out whether there was mention of either a Henry or a Ruth Webbe amongst the signatures on the study wall. The next morning I studied the wall closely, and although I could not find a Ruth Webbe, I did find the inscription,

'Henry Webbe, my house 1678.'

It seemed possible therefore, that a Henry Webbe *had* lived in the house during the 1670s.

After that night I was never disturbed again. It seemed I had released whatever was trapped. The next morning I decided that it would be interesting to find out through automatic writing if Millicent Webbe knew of Robert Webbe's father,

Richard. Obviously she would not know Robert, I thought, unless they had both met each other later. . . .

'Richard Uncle. Yes I know Uncle Richard he is angry with me. Help me. Please for me Pray or must I always suffer. Forgive my sins. I killed my baby and now I am taken. Sing mass for me I beg.'

'Do you know Robert Webbe? He is the son of Richard' I asked her.

'Robert. No I do not know of Robert. Richards children are honourabel + Little Richard John and Sarah are they. Please forgive me. Pray. Millicent Webbe.'

To begin with it was not easy to understand what she meant as her language was not very lucid. I deduced, however, from that statement, that Richard Webbe's children, up to the time Millicent died in 1670, were Richard, John and Sarah.

In 1971 when I had asked Robert Webbe about his family, he had told me that his father, Richard, had died in 1703, and that Richard's children (Robert's brothers and sisters) were Richard, John, Sarah and Elizabeth.

The names that Millicent gave me were the same as the names Robert Webbe gave me, except that Millicent does not include Elizabeth and Robert. Maybe, I decided, they were born after she had died. When asked if she knew of Richard Webbe, she had referred to him as 'Uncle', implying that perhaps Richard was Henry's brother. As Robert Webbe claimed to have been born in the house in 1678, it seems a reasonable assumption that the two brothers and their respective families shared the house together, unless the information contained in the various automatic scripts is inaccurate.

Interestingly, Robert Webbe claimed in automatic writing to have heard of Millicent, when on 14th February, 1974, I asked him about her.

'Indeede do I knowe of her. She brought so much bad name to the Webbes but she died in birth before me. They say that her sewter was the young rascal Casbolt.'

It seemed that the Webbes had not forgotten the shame that they saw Millicent as having brought to their name. Checking

DISCOURSES

ON THE

FOLLOWING SUBJECTS:

I. The Use of the Law. | III. The Effect of the Grace of God upon the Hearts and Lives of Professors.
II. The Insufficiency of the Creature, &c. and the All-sufficiency of Christ. | IV, V, VI The Parable of the Sower.

By the Rev. SAMUEL HICKS,
Rector of Wrestlingworth in Bedfordshire.

LONDON,

Printed for the AUTHOR,
By J. and W. Oliver, in Bartholomew Close, near West Smithfield;
And Sold by G. Keith, in Grace-church Street,
E. and C. Dilly, in the Poultry,
and by Messrs Merrit, in Cambridge.

...ing more than means still. The supper, instruct and continuance of the spiritual life are here our being.

Why, Doctor, you talk most amazingly of Jesus Christ: I never heard the like before. Some people only vamp him up as a prophet, and trample on his blood: and some, who do not like to hear of hell, shew a Jewish heart, and call him an impostor; but you make him God Almighty, our Creator and Preserver and Redeemer. Truly, I would give him all his due, but must have his honours fetched from the holy Bible, and not from human brains. My bosom sweeps away all cobwebs, whether spun by a spider or the doctor. Give me some fair and plain account of Jesus Christ from the scripture: I love the Bible, and can credit what it says.

Now you talk like a man, Sir: when you lifted up your staff before, I begun to think of packing up my alls. A cudgel is too hard — argument for me. But since you ask Bible, I am well content to stay. And what it says of Jesus Christ. Before human nature, he created all things — vine power, all matter, and all animal spirits human or angelic. St. John charges on St. John's words, sayan things were made by him: John i. were created by him, that are in be are in earth, visible and invisible: a

10. Pages of one of the books presented to us by Webbe. On the flyleaf it can be seen that the book was originally sold in Cambridge by Messrs Merrit.

11. 'My house was bilt by one William Crutchley . . . and completed ye July 1731.' A hopper head on the side of Queens House.

the signatures on the wall, I found two Casbolts—'John Casbolt 1696' and 'Richard Casbolt 1702'. Millicent's signature does not appear on the wall.

Later I communicated further in automatic writing with Millicent Webbe, trying to find out information about her family, and gradually I discovered that she seemed considerably more lucid than her cousin, Robert. Eventually I extracted more data from her than I had done from Robert Webbe about her family. She was never willing to write about her life, as Robert had been, and she seemed genuinely aware of her plight in contrast to Robert Webbe who was reliving his past life in cycles.

The first of the lengthy communications I had with Millicent occurred on February 18th, 1974.

'Who were your brothers and sisters, and how old are they in 1670?' I asked.

'I am Millicent. Also is there Henry who is XXV at West Wykham. John XXIX. Phillip and Ruth and Thomas who all live in the churchyarde. Also with me James XXVII and Katherine XIX and Rachel XIII.'

'When and where did your parents marry?'

'Just in MDCXLI at Lynton.'

'What was the family name of your mother before she married?' I asked.

'Grandfather Jordan. Ruth Jordan of Lynton,' Millicent wrote.

'What was the occupation of your grandfather?'

'A wodeyard had he.'

'What was the occupation of your father?'

'Henry is farmer. Why ask of me all so many names. Pray for me. Millicent.'

'How old is your father?' I continued.

'MDCXX,' was the reply.

'How old is your mother?'

'MDCXXIII.'

'When did your father die?'

'Came he to the churchyarde in MDCLXXIX. Ruth MDCLXXIX.'

'I want to know about your family because I am interested,' I wrote, sensing that she was getting bored with answering apparently pointless questions about her family.

'I do not see. We are not of Paris bloode. We are symple here. I am onley Millicent Webbe,' she wrote, as if surprised that anybody should be interested in her ordinary country family. It struck me that Robert Webbe would never write that—he would tell me how his family were the most important in Linton.

'Who is the King?' I asked her.

'They tell Charles II.'

'How many people lived in your house?'

'Henry and Ruth and John Phillip Ruth Tho: James Katherine Millicent are we.'

'Did anybody else live here with you?' I asked, remembering my idea about the house having been shared by two families.

'Too: Richard and his wyfe Mary who lives in churchyarde and now Penelope and all there children: Richard John Eliz: Sarah and I see Rob: and more in churchyard too. Rob: Richard is brother of Henry all of one house. And too low down lane Phillip but not my brother and his Anne and children five. Phillip Sam: Anne Sarah and Susannah.'

'What was the occupation of Phillip?' I asked her.

'Phillip makes shos,' she answered.

It seemed that Millicent was now also claiming that there had been two children of Richard Webbe, both named Robert, as he had claimed himself, so I asked her why there were two Roberts.

'I live in churchyarde but stil I have seen two Rob: Two twyns but one dead soon. Two boys twyns. Both Rob: because one deade,' was her explanation.

All her information was fascinating once it was unravelled. It seemed that there really were two quite different personalities contained in the automatic writings of Robert and Millicent Webbe.

Millicent seemed child-like and innocent, almost naive,

while Robert Webbe was full of confidence, self-importance and magniloquence.

According to Millicent then, her parents, Henry and Ruth, were married in Linton in 1641, aged twenty-one and nineteen respectively. They had nine children: John born in 1641, James born in 1643, Henry born in 1645, Katherine born in 1651, then Millicent born in 1655 and Rachel born in 1657. I presumed that Phillip, Ruth and Thomas 'who live all in churchyarde' were children who died during infancy. Out of those nine children, it would seem that only five survived beyond the age of fifteen. Millicent's parents died in 1671 and 1679, her father being aged 57 and her mother aged only 55, if her information can be trusted, because she claims to have died herself in 1670, before either of her parents.

The house, according to Millicent's information, was shared by the family of Henry's brother Richard, who had six children. It would also seem, that somewhere close was a cottage in which lived a Phillip Webbe.

Her reference to being 'not of Paris bloode' is particularly interesting, although before I received Millicent's message I already knew of the Paris family because there is a large monumental tomb of theirs inside Linton church, and some of their names were included on the study wall. They were the largest family in Linton and lived in the Manor House.

Her reference to people who lived in the churchyard was a childish euphemism for saying that they were dead. Maybe, to cushion the effect of frequent deaths, Millicent and her brothers and sisters were told that people went to live in the churchyard.

I then decided to ask Millicent about the brothers and sisters of her parents.

'Did your father have any brothers and sisters, and do you know when they were born?', was my first question.

'Of Thomas and Katherine Webbe Tho: Richard Katherine Henry William Ann.'

'Do you know who any of these children married?'

'Tho: lives in churchyarde.

'Richard and Hannah.
'Katherine in churchyarde.
'Henry and Ruth Jordan.
'Will. and Lettice.
'Ann and Barnabas Paye.'

I thought by now that I had gained almost enough information to make a family tree of the Webbes from Millicent's writings alone. Much of it seemed to correspond with what Robert Webbe had told me. I was rather puzzled, though, that Millicent had now said that Richard, her father's brother, married Hannah, because previously she had said that he had married twice, first to Mary and then to Penelope.

'Are you sure that Richard, the brother of Henry, married Hannah?' I asked her.

I waited for a few moments before she wrote,

'This Rich: maried Mary and Penelope. Rich: brother of Phill. married Hannah.'

Phillip was supposed to have been the shoemaker who lived near to the house.

'Whose son is Phillip?' I asked her.

'The son of Will. and Lettice,' she wrote automatically.

'Who were all the children of William and Lettice Webbe?' I asked.

'Will: Phill: Rich: Lettice: Susannah: Henrietta: Eliz: John: Anne: Sarah: James: Tho:' she spelled out laboriously.

I thought that the next question I wanted to ask her was rather difficult for a fifteen-year-old girl. I was wrong.

'Do you know who were the brothers and sisters of your grandfather, Thomas Webbe?'

'Of John Webbe and Eliz his wyfe of Bartlow John Henry Eliz: Tho: Mary Edward.'

When I began to combine and compare the information I had received in automatic writing from both Millicent and Robert Webbe, I noticed discrepancies in the information they had given.

In one of Robert's earlier writings he had claimed that his grandfather was Henry Webbe. According to Millicent, however, Thomas Webbe was the father of both Richard and Henry, the occupants of the house whilst Millicent was alive.

Other interesting facts emerged from their writings: between them, three of Thomas Webbe's sons, namely Henry, William and Richard, fathered twenty-seven children. Was it surprising, therefore, I wondered, that Millicent and Robert Webbe so frequently became confused when asked about their family? I also worked out that if this information was correct, there were at least thirty Webbes all living on one site in two houses. It also meant that over the years Robert Webbe must have had twenty-six cousins! I began to wonder what so many Webbes could have done for a living—obviously they were not all country gentlemen. But I knew already that Phillip was a shoemaker.

I asked Millicent what her father's occupation was.

'Pigs and some gotes and some grain,' she replied.

'What does he do with his animals and the grain?'

'They are solde. Richard sells in shoppe.'

If she was to be believed, it seemed that the two brothers were in business together. Henry farmed, and Richard sold the produce. Robert Webbe presumably took over his father's business later on, which makes sense because he had described his occupation as a 'trader of grain'—a corn merchant.

During this time I had been surprised at the intelligence of Millicent, especially compared to Robert, and at her clear handwriting, which again was a contrast with Robert's. One day I asked her where she had learned to read and write, since she appeared to be educated.

'Mr. Thomas Punter and lately none,' she replied.

I had heard of Thomas Punter's name before, and his signature was on the wall, dated 1666, and signed with a cross. In Linton Parish Church is a board containing all the names of the past Vicars of Linton. From that I discovered that Punter was Vicar of Linton from 1649 to 1660, and then again from 1663 to 1685.

After several weeks it seemed as if Millicent was a reservoir which I had emptied. I could now sit for long periods of time trying to get her to write automatically, but with no success. She seemed to have gone, although we never had prayers said for her as she had requested. I had noticed, though, that I had never had another disturbed night while sleeping in my bedroom, since I had communicated with her.

Before she emerged, or rather before I became aware of her, I had noticed that Robert Webbe had become very inactive, almost as if he had been eclipsed by another planet. I now think that he was aware of Millicent, and he was jealous of her because he wanted all the attention. As soon as Millicent faded, he returned with a final vengeance.

I was sad to have lost Millicent, although we never really treated her in the same way as we had treated Robert. We never regarded her as a 'person', more of a harmless ghost, which was after all what she was. She was a source of coherent information. Robert Webbe had always been, and remained, erratic, even at the best of times.

Robert Webbe was interesting because he was unpredictable—almost like a bull who would snort and charge if he saw red.

# Eight:    'My departure is nigh'

Robert Webbe may have quietened down, but he had not yet left his house completely. He was still interested in what was happening, and in the objects he found belonging to us.

After seeing him on the second occasion, I had drawn a more detailed sketch illustrating the clothes I had seen him wearing. (He was wearing exactly the same clothes as he had worn on the first occasion I saw him.) It was by no means a drawing of artistic merit, but it was better than the sketch I had made when I first saw him on the stairs. It lacked the spontaneity of my first sketch because, I suppose, it was premeditated. When it was finished, I left it with the original sketch, on top of a thick pile of Robert Webbe's automatic writings in a large polythene bag which lay on the study table. Later in the day I returned to collect the bag which I intended putting elsewhere, with other material relating to Robert Webbe.

Picking up the bag I quickly grabbed the second sketch I had recently drawn, from the other end of the table, placing it in the bag with the other papers. Then I realized that I had already placed it in the bag before, earlier in the day. I thought somebody had probably been looking at it.

I glanced at the drawing through the plastic bag and noticed that somebody had written 'Rob:Webbe 1733' across the top of it, apparently with my own fountain pen which had also been left on the table. I put down the bag and removed the drawing to inspect it more closely. It looked very much as though Robert Webbe himself had signed the drawing—it was his handwriting and not that of any member of the family.

Finding a sheet of clean paper, I wrote across the top of it:

'Thank you for signing your name on the picture of yourself.'

It was the first time for many months that I had communicated with him in automatic writing. He seemed overjoyed at
the opportunity I had offered him.

' 'Tis a moste noble effort and bears goode likeness to me,'
he enthused. 'I should be very humble for another for my goode
selfe.'

I then decided to look inside the bag to see if Webbe had
written anything on my original sketch. I sorted through all
his automatic writings over and over again searching for it. I
was unable to find it, although I quite clearly remembered having seen it earlier in the day. It had vanished, and was never
seen again. Fortunately, there were photocopies of it in existence, but they were naturally inferior to the original. My first
sketch had so many strange and incredible memories associated
with it which a copy could never recapture. Funnily enough,
if I was asked which article I should most like to have returned
to me from the selection of vanished belongings from the house,
I would choose that sketch. The other articles could be replaced
but the sketch was unique.

I was not sure how Robert Webbe thought I was going to
produce a copy for him; may be he had visions of me carefully
drawing a replica. Instead, I had it photocopied and a few days
later told him that I had the copy he had asked for.

'I shall leave it at the top of the stairs for you,' I told him.

'I must proclaim moste hearty thanks for it. I shall look well
on it. I very much fancey it,' he exclaimed.

The photocopy was duly left lying at the top of the stairs one
evening at about eight o'clock. Nobody thought any more of
it until we saw it lying there three hours later as we went to
bed.

Some time during the night the drawing disappeared and has
never been seen again. Ironically it seemed that I had given
Robert Webbe some kind of key with which he could unlock
the doors which had trapped him in the house since 1733.
Almost as if he was now content in the knowledge that somebody had finally noticed and recognized him, this thought
being embodied in the drawing of him, he seemed to have made

a conscious effort to 'rest in peace'. From that time hence, the unending and strange phenomena we had come to associate with him subsided. They did not disappear completely—they just became less intense.

It was as though he saw the sketch as a mirror into which he looked with horror, suddenly asking himself what he was doing. He seemed to become aware at last that he was in the wrong place. It was as if he realized that he should not be in the house, which really did belong not to him, but to us.

Of course, he did not vacate the house completely, or immediately, because from time to time strange things have still occurred, albeit with less of their previous intensity. We were less aware of sudden strange smells, odd noises, alien objects, and most of all of his spontaneous automatic writing.

His writings did not suddenly cease like a spring which dries up. It was as though previously I had been his secretary, producing a constant flow of automatic writing from the reservoir of Webbe's consciousness and memory. Now that reservoir seemed to have been drained because the tap only released small, intermittent trickles of brackish, unpalatable water, clouded by swirling mud which had lain on the bottom of the reservoir.

His later communications displayed a consuming preoccupation with his ill-health, and the state of his legs. He seemed to grow more confused, as if he had become exhausted trying to swim away from his spiritual shipwreck. Finally they appeared to be merely transcripts of monologues he was holding with himself.

'You can do nowt for my legs. Indeed I feare they may soon be severed from my very body. Try and comfort my poor wife Mary who weeps every morning in my bedchamber as my legs rotte before our eyes. She knowes I will surely die. I stand at the top of the stairs when my departure is nigh.'

Most of the final automatic writings were in that vein and I had a growing impression of a man terrified by approaching death, as if he envisaged death as a chained skeleton who would come clanking into his bedroom at night to carry him away.

*113*

He was fighting illusions, making occasional grabs for reality before he disappeared under the waves. The only way he could hold onto what he saw as reality was to swim for the island he could see in the water. It was that island, his house, which became his refuge.

'Today my legs are moste bad and I feare I shall soon die,' he would scrawl.

'I must wander for the maladies and wretched sores upon my legs. Some days my legs are so mighty painful I can scarce walk to my room.'

'And the blessed legs so badde I have to walk myne house at nite.'

'I died in 1733 from my troublesome legs.'

His legs became his chief preoccupation, a growing obsession.

The last automatic writings that I received from him ignored the plight of his legs, but it was rather as though I was tuning in to a mind tortured by the gap between reality and unreality, because the messages made so little sense. He appeared to be answering questions which I had not put to him, which was why I had decided that he was holding monologues with himself.

'I often talke with you by myne writing and I feare I am tiresome saying so little. One day I must see maney persons, but now I am not to. A mightey bothersome sticke in myne pathway, blessed rodd. A poore stride on myne poore legg. A fine job too. I know no such man but a Phillip Harvey of Lynton.'

One of the last cogent messages I received from him came at Christmas in 1974, but it was not from the Robert Webbe we had all come to know. He had lost his humour and the sparkle had finally gone.

'It is moste certainly true to say that the Festive Seasonne approaches close. Remember therefore at this time that the strictest and most scrupulous honour and virtue can alone make you esteemed and valued by mankind. There is an awkwardness of expressionne and wordes moste carefully to be avoided; such as false English bad pronunciation, old sayings and common proverbs, which are to many proof of having kept bad and low company,' he preached.

He may have been more lucid at this point than he had been for some months previously, but this was not the usual Robert Webbe, the man who loved to indulge and enjoy himself. He had never before written in such a puritanical fashion.

I am sure that in some symbolic way, the photocopy of my sketch which he removed from the staircase, was the event which changed his attitude. He had never been the same after that. From a selfish point of view it was sad that he had apparently gone at last, even if he did return for an occasional visit, as if to see how we were managing without him. When he had gone we all started to ask questions of each other and ourselves too.

For how long had he haunted the house? Why did he first haunt it? Had it been my presence in particular which had brought him back to 'life'? Why had he gone away now? Of course there were more banal questions as well—we wondered how many belongings we had lost, and what they could be. Where were they now?

I cannot say why he chose to haunt this house, or why he has sporadically returned but I have some ideas which have occurred to me over the years as a result of my experience with him.

Robert Webbe had spent his entire life consolidating his business and his trade. He wanted to be even more successful than his father and his overriding ambition was to create a monument which would show others how successful he had been in materialistic terms. In 1731, therefore, he had had built at quite considerable expense the front of the house which was intricately panelled in moulded pine throughout, and contained a fine carved pine staircase.

Less than eighteen months later he had died, fighting to the last for his life and enjoying for so short a time what he had successfully created for himself and his family. He was not terrified of dying so much; he was aware that death was no respecter of persons. He was terrified of leaving his house—had it been possible he would have taken it away to live in, for it was the village symbol of his wealth and his success. I believe he was unaware of the spiritual nature of an existence after physical death; I expect that he imagined that life would continue somewhere else when it had been concluded here in Linton. He would still be Robert Webbe, Gentleman, a wealthy merchant.

Maybe after he died, he glimpsed a new existence and quickly struggled back against a receding tide, to remain amongst his material surroundings where, he believed, nothing would change.

Things did change, however, and this time he was wrong. Time passed him by, and people unknown to him moved into his house, taking away his possessions. He was stranded, unable to make any of the incumbents aware of his existence in the house, or of his plight, apart from being able to wander about, occasionally removing interesting objects which caught his eye. Everyone he knew gradually vanished.

He had barely left his house since the time he died in 1733. Because of his materialistic desires, he had become the prisoner of infinity; and the fact that, later, he saw an alternative existence made no allowance for the fact that he had money and was a gentleman. He had no wish to be on the same level as everybody else. He remained in Queen's House, experiencing *déjà vu* scenes of his physical life in the eighteenth century without any awareness of time. The centrifugal existence into which he had hobbled on his two sticks was without a time scale. It was as if he was watching a continuous loop of film of his physical life and somebody was causing the speed of the projector to accelerate and then slow down.

Had Robert Webbe always been 'active' in the house, or was it merely my presence which had activated him? I believe that he made his presence felt in varying degrees, depending on who was resident in the house. I think it is quite possible that a certain number of people who occupied the house at various times between 1733 and 1971 (when we first became aware of Robert Webbe's presence) acted as 'batteries', supplying him with the necessary energy to sustain his restlessness and activity. Perhaps

when somebody with a psychic temperament was living in the
house, he would be more active than if the house was occupied
by somebody who was not such a good 'energy supply'. I
evolved this idea after I had received in automatic writing a
message from Webbe at a time when I was in a different part
of the country. He wrote,

'I indeed perceive the light to have been extinguished from
near me. You are no more and my spirit thirsts for the light
of you. I can see you no longer and I am powerless at rest once
more tho' I still walk at my hour at night.'

It was as if Webbe himself envisaged *me* more as a light in
the house, illuminating the area in which he existed. Without
light, he could not do much more than walk.

I also noticed another feature concerning all the apports,
which would appear to confirm my idea. Most could, with few
exceptions, be placed in four distinct time groups between the
eighteenth and twentieth centuries. I believe that each of the
apports originated from previous occupants of the house, and
that the owners of the objects in each of these groups supplied
Robert Webbe with the energy, psychic or otherwise, which
allowed him to 'function'. (It may not necessarily have been
the owner who was the energy donor, but perhaps somebody
else living in the house at the same time, especially children
who are frequently known to be the centres of poltergeist
activity, for example.)

One group of apports, the geological specimens (including
the fossilized fern leaf, the piece of iron pyrites, and the polished
granite pebble), originated quite possibly from one source. I
expect that there was somebody in the house who collected geological specimens. Another group of apports would all fit quite
happily into a household from the latter part of the eighteenth
century; into this group I would place the two leather-bound
books, the beeswax candle, the bottle neck, the cork bung and
the two loaves. During the 1940s, I expect that one inhabitant
would find that he or she had lost a sixpence in mint condition
and dated 1942, the strange typewritten letter, dated 1948, the
plastic beads, and a pair of white nylon gloves which we found.

(It is possible that Webbe mistook these for a pair of kid gloves.) The fourth group would include the objects that we have lost during the time we have lived in the house.

From this point of view, therefore, I think the fact that Robert Webbe became active while I was living in the house, is to a certain extent irrelevant. Anybody of a psychic temperament had the potential ability to affect him in the way in which my presence acted as a catalyst.

I cannot say whether Robert Webbe will ever return in the way that he lived again between 1971 and 1974, but I feel that he is a 'spent force'. He may still be here, but only as an empty reservoir. If the most psychically gifted person in the world were to live for years in the house, I do not think that they could energize Webbe sufficiently to produce the same phenomena that we experienced during those three years. I like to think that Robert Webbe became more aware of his situation through his communication with me and that, as a result of this, he has passed to a more acceptable level of post-mortal existence. Since 1974 the house has been strangely tranquil, bereft of the activities we associated so readily with him; as if a storm had passed.

Perhaps, during that storm, Robert Webbe was swept off his island and was able to reach the shore he had been destined for in 1733.

It was another of those halcyon days during the hot summers we have experienced recently: one of those days on which it seemed that nothing strange could happen. After all, strange phenomena are traditionally associated with windswept, creaky houses in the middle of nowhere, and occur on bleak, winter nights. But this was different. The brilliant sunlight swept through the windows, its light falling in broken patterns on the carpeted floor of the bedroom.

On consideration, everything in that room seemed to exist in a timeless realm. The shadows cast by the glazing bars of the window had not changed at all since the house had been built nearly two hundred and fifty years before. The floor was carpeted now and perhaps the boards were bare then.

In fact, this morning reminded me of that day, which now seemed so distant, when we had discovered the strange eighteenth-century signatures written on the panelled walls. Three years ago seemed to me so very distant. I wondered how long it seemed to Robert Webbe. Life continued though, as it had done for uncounted generations in Queen's House.

But something had changed that morning—although it probably passed undetected by most of my family. Something was different.

During the years since that fateful day in 1733, two time scales had been running parallel to each other in the house. There was our own time scale (which must be the right one, surely?) and there was also another one in which Robert Webbe had been existing.

Now there is only one time scale which is real, and that is our own. The other has been absorbed by history, and has seeped back into the bricks of the house, and the pages of books which recorded those times.

That morning we found something I had given to Robert Webbe when I met him for the second time, in the upstairs bedroom. On my parents' bed lay a miniature wooden clog.

# Nine: Epilogue

One afternoon, on May 15th, 1977, I felt a sudden compulsion to communicate once more with Robert Webbe; I did not know what to expect as it was nearly two years since I had last had any messages from him. I was not sure if he would be preoccupied with the state of his health or whether he would be willing to communicate if he was still around. As events occurred it seemed that the long break had restored some semblance of rationality to Webbe's thinking. Having completed my research in the Cambridgeshire County Records Office, I had a number of questions to ask Robert Webbe.

The resulting dialogue in automatic writing between myself and Robert Webbe placed me in a quandary: the information it contained was, I felt, the most fascinating material that I had ever received automatically. I knew that it had to be included in this book but there was no place where it would fit conveniently whilst still making sense. For this reason I have reproduced the 'conversation' that occurred by itself in this separate appendix.

It began with Robert Webbe writing.

'Indeede a mightey fine daye and off to myne man Rob: Moore for a fine goodley meel with myne wyfe. And just too Church today and a boring sermon. Didst tickel myne fancey to have a taste of licker in the sermon. And myne man Browne is such a fool. Just last week did he lose his roofe to flames. A mightey fyne fire. I didst stand and watch but not to close lest my pretty wig be lycked by the flames.'

'What date is it today?' I asked him.

'Indeede I perceeve ye date to be ye 23rd. May 1726 and
a fyne white day too. And you cannot see me but I am here.
I am Robert Webbe. And I am a gentleman.'

'Are there any other gentlemen in Linton?'

'Rob: Webbe is a Gent. And also there are other good
upright men to. But I have many shops. They have onley there
houses and there servants. They all by there corn and grain
from me. So I am Rob: Webbe.'

'What do you do all day?' I asked.

'I sell my goodes to ye millers and all farmers who bye grain
for there animals. And I go to Cambridge to sell my grayne.
Mostly they come to me. But sometimes I spend all day long
in myne house. I smoke and I drink and it is not good for myne
mynde says wyfe. But what for I ask? I shall soon perish and
wither like a flower. But the Rector talks of God and of the
hereafter but tis not for me. I do not beleeve in angels or other
strumpets. I am Rob: Webbe.'

'What do you believe happens after you die?' I enquired.

'They lay you in the ground and you are consumed by the
worms. It is black and all is spent (?). There are no angels and
devils really. I say such topics are for ye children too make them
goode. But what good is it for one such as me? I live here and
I am not to be beleeving such tales. I go to Church but if I
do not who byes my grayne. I here them then say that I am
an evill man not of God. But when I die it is the end. I do
not want to perish. I am Rob: Webbe.'

'Do you believe in ghosts?'

'Such topics are for ye olde women. Of course ghosts are
never so. And such tripe. But I would not care to meet a ghost.
It is said they live in Churchyardes at nite so I keep away.'

'Why do you keep away from the churchyard if you do not
believe in ghosts?' I asked him.

'I am fearefull of such things. I wish not to see one,' he replied.

'Have you ever seen a ghost?' I wrote.

'No I believe not. And goode too.'

'What would you do if you *did* see one?' I asked him.

'I would tell it that it was not real and that I was Robert Webbe.'

'Are there ghosts in your house?' I asked, beginning to realize that some fascinating material was likely to be written if I asked the right questions.

'Of course not else I would chase them away,' he quickly replied.

'We live in your house now and we have seen a ghost here.'

'I do not believe such tales. You try to frighten me out.'

'The ghost we have seen wears breeches, stockings, a long coat, waistcoat, and wig. He has two sticks and appears on the stairs,' I informed him.

'But I never see any ghost in myne house. Do you speak with this ghoull or is it dumb?' He asked apparently completely unaware that I was referring to *him*.

'We speak with it,' I told him.

'But how speke you with it if it is dead? The dead cannot talk. But tell me a litle of what this ghoul says.'

'He tells us that he lived in this house and that he died in 1733.'

'This cannot be so,' he replied indignantly in automatic writing. 'I live here if 'tis 1733. And I am not a ghoul. I am Rob: Webbe. And tell me what this ghost is called?'

'He calls himself Robert Webbe,' I told him.

'But this cannot be. I am Rob:Webbe. You have a man who cheets you. I am Rob:W. And you have too someone who likes to be me. Off with you. I am here and I am me,' he retorted obviously becoming a little bewildered, if not frightened.

'Who do you think you are talking to?' I asked him.

'I thinks sometimes I am going mad. I hear a voyce in myne head which I hear talking to me and asking me what I do. But tell no one else they locke me away. Who is this voice?'

'The voice is me. Who am I?' I asked him. I had the distinct feeling of meeting somebody in a dark room after believing that I was alone in the room. It was very peculiar.

'You frighten me. Who are you? You talk to me in myne head. I go madde then. I only here you in myne heade and

Epilogue

not in myne ears. Who are you? Are you the ghost this voyce
talks of?'

'I am alive, and I live in your house. You are dead,' I told
him.

'This is nonsense,' was his predictable response. 'I am alive
because I am here. If you are the voyce you are the ghost and
you are dead. I cannot be deade else I would not be here,' he
replied. I was beginning to wonder how I could think that I
was more logical than Webbe. It was becoming rather surreal-
istic.

'You died in 1736. I read this in the Parish Registers. The
Vicar writes that he buried Robert Webbe, Gent. in April,
1736.' It was as though I was a policeman trying to force a
confession out of a criminal by presenting him with incriminat-
ing facts!

'Then the goode man is deceved by his eyes. Why I saw him
onley today. How is this if he buried me. I must have words
with him.'

'I think that you are a ghost and that you died 250 years
ago,' I replied.

'You are mistaken,' he insisted. 'I am no ghoste. I am here.
You frighten me. And who do you say you are'.

'My name is Matthew Manning and my family live in your
house.'

'But this I cannot understand. Where came you from? I have
not sold myne house.'

'We bought it in 1968,' I told him.

'Now you jeste. It is only 1726 and you tell me tis 1968. Tis
a joke. Are you a ghoulle of tomorrow? Off with you. Rob:
Webbe is mad. Mad. Mad.'

'You have talked to me before. What do you think I look
like?'

'I here onley this voyce in myne head. I cannot see you. But
I here this voyce for many years now and I know I go madd.
Do not tell others. You are me if you are in myne head.'

I believe that this message shows clearly how Robert Webbe
sees himself in relation to death, time, and myself more than

*123*

any other message I have received from him. It is apparent that he still believes himself to be physically alive in 1726; I suspect that he is quite aware of his physical demise since he has made reference to it on two occasions but prefers to reject the truth. Even at this stage he still continues to believe that he is alive and living in Linton in 1726. However, after reading this message several times I wondered how I could be so certain that my perception of reality was more valid than that of Robert Webbe.

Various thoughts came to my mind as I tried to fit the various phenomena associated with Webbe into some framework of explanation: is all time simultaneous, there being no such thing as past, present, and future? After all, time is essentially man-made and perhaps there is a certain level of reality of which we are normally unaware on which everything is occurring simultaneously. Perhaps there are many levels of reality all coexisting simultaneously although normally we are quite unaware of any alternative states of reality. Maybe Robert Webbe *is* still alive, living in 'our' house and continuing with his everyday life just as we do; perhaps his perception of reality is not the same as ours. The appearance of Robert Webbe in an apparent physical form, the apport phenomenon, and the experience of my father when Webbe, lying in the same bed appears to be superimposed over my father's physical body, may be what I would call 'time slips' when one dimension of reality overlaps another by some process of distortion. Maybe the reader will form his or her own theories on the matter.

However, it was the references made by Robert Webbe to hearing voices in his head that I found most fascinating as it was quite evident that Webbe had no idea with whom he was communicating. He believed he was going mad because he heard voices in his head asking him questions. Although he had communicated many thousands of words to me over a six-year period he was quite unaware that there was any real communication occurring. Furthermore he was apparently quite unaware that he had appeared as a ghost in the house and had no recollection of having met me on two occasions although

I had spoken to him at each meeting. This suggests that my previous contention that he was reliving certain scenes from his life over and over again may be correct. Maybe if he crosses from one plane of reality to another he has no recollection of having done so.

The most powerful question asked by Webbe at any time was, 'Are you a ghoulle of tomorrow?'

Although I regard Robert Webbe's story to have a moral to it, maybe it raises a more interesting question:

Are we already ghosts to somebody else?

# *Appendix 1:*    *The Final Twist*

After I finished writing *The Strangers*, in late 1976, I was reluctant to start doing my own research on the material contained in Robert Webbe's automatic writing, despite the fact that, because he had made a number of categorical statements, I thought it would not be difficult to corroborate what he said.

There were a number of reasons for my reluctance. I felt strongly that *The Strangers* was essentially a fascinating *story* which would be spoiled by research. I would have been quite happy for a historian to do the research and to then write a report which I could use as an appendix to the book. But my publishers were against this idea, saying that I should do my own research.

I was aware that if I was to do this, I should be laying myself open to attack from critics who would suggest that I had looked up the information first, and then attributed it to Robert Webbe. Gradually I accepted that those critics would try to debunk the story in any case, regardless of whether it was researched by myself, or not researched at all.

Perhaps my strongest reason for not wishing to compare the facts in the automatic writing with contemporary records was an intangible one. Robert Webbe was a person, not only to myself, but to the rest of the family; we all had an 'image' of him which was in danger of being destroyed by the 'reality' of contemporary records. There was also something warning me not to research the story—maybe it was the influence of Robert Webbe.

Eventually I was persuaded by my publishers to do some work on trying to verify the information in the automatic writing.

## Appendix 1

And so that was how I came to arrive at the Cambridgeshire County Records Office, where *The Strangers* began to grow into a fascinating detective story with an amazing twist which was to surprise everybody. Most detective stories begin with a crime and several suspects who are slowly eliminated until only the culprit remains. As far as *The Strangers* was concerned it was the other way round. I worked from the premise that I was looking for evidence to incriminate one culprit, which is never a wise thing to do I suppose, and in the process I began to reveal another suspect.

During all the years that I had been communicating with Robert Webbe, I had been under the impression that I was communicating with only one person. It never occurred to me that he might not have been alone. Apart from anything else, the Robert Webbe that I had *seen* had always been the same person—or at least seemed to have been, but perhaps I was wrong...

I am well aware that the narrative which emerges from the automatic writing, and other experiences associated with Queen's House, is weird and at times verging on the bizarre. I am also aware that it is in parts inconsistent, although still humanly possible.

The inconsistency that seemed the most puzzling concerned the tradesmen's tokens. When questioned about their disappearance, Robert Webbe had replied, 'I must use such tokens ...'

The latest date on any of the four tokens is 1667, and as my father observed at the time, they would have been in use for about five years at the most at the time of their issue; certainly they would never have been in circulation much later than ten to fifteen years after they were first issued. If, as Robert Webbe claimed, he was born in 1678, would they really have been of any use to him, especially as he apparently believed that he was living between 1726 and 1733? And since Robert Moore was one of the tradesmen from whom a token originated, was it really likely that Robert Webbe would have apparently known him so well? These are just two inconsistencies which are immediately obvious. Maybe whilst reading this book, you have stopped to consider other apparent anomalies.

After I had completed my research, which took me to the County Records Offices of Cambridgeshire and Essex, the Cambridge University Library, and Saffron Walden Parish Church, I concluded that I was dealing with two gentlemen, both named Robert Webbe. If this really was the case, all the inconsistencies could be explained, especially if one realizes that these two gentlemen spanned between them a period from about 1664 to 1736. I shall explain this more fully later. At this point I shall merely refer to the two men as Robert Webbe senior and Robert Webbe junior.

Now, studying the automatic scripts more closely I noticed that there were two quite distinct and different handwritings that even my graphologically untrained eye could observe. I suppose that if I had noticed this previously I had put it down to different moods etc. that I had been in at the time. I also noticed that any one script refers to either the house as it is now, as Robert junior built it, or the back part only, as Robert senior would have known it before the front was added. Those messages where there are references to 'my parlour' (which would have been in the older section of the house) consistently refer to historical dates of earlier periods.

Maybe the most curious aspect of this apparent twist to the story is that no reference was made by either senior or junior Webbe that either of them was aware of the other's presence in the house. However, both saw me as a stranger—in fact all the family were strangers. They were also strangers to each other in death, and strangers to us as occupants of their house. It would seem that the house was the only factor common to both of them in their post-mortal existence.

*The Strangers*, a title I had chosen for the book before I began my research, suddenly seemed more apt than ever.

Before I began my research I made a list of 'facts' which Robert Webbe had included in his automatic scripts between 1971 and 1975; I then placed the correct information, according to contemporary records, next to Webbe's information. A table, which initially puzzled and disturbed me, began to grow exceedingly interesting.

Perhaps half of Webbe's information *was* correct according to various contemporary documents, but what worried me was that the other half was, to say the least, far from accurate. Rather than concentrate on the information which was immediately corroborated, I became fascinated by the information that conflicted with original documents. Why, I wondered, should half of the information be totally correct, while the other half was very inaccurate?

My research had begun with a large volume of hand-written entries documenting all the baptisms, marriages, and burials of Linton villagers known as the Linton Parish Register. I chose as a starting point for my research the date at which Robert Webbe claimed to have been born.

'I was born in 1678,' he had written.

I searched unsuccessfully for a reference to his baptism in that year; neither could I find any record of his baptism in the years immediately following. It was not until I reached the year 1686 that I found this entry: 'Robert of Robert and Penelope Webb, July 15.'

This statement of fact contradicted two other facts that Robert Webbe had written automatically. Firstly, there was a difference of eight years in the dates of birth, and secondly, he had written previously: 'My father was Richard Webbe, Gent. who died in 1703.'

What was I to believe: the automatic writings or the original documents? Before I gave this any further thought, I decided to complete my research.

Having attempted to untangle the mystery of Webbe's birth-date, I next checked his date of death in the burial section of the Parish Registers. There was no mention at all of a Robert Webbe having died in 1733. I discovered, however, that he was buried on April 4th, 1736, which was three years later than the latest date that Robert Webbe had ever signed with his name at the end of an automatic message.

Often he had told me: 'I died in 1733 of my troublesome legs.'

I have no positive explanation for the apparent discrepancies in the dates of his birth and death. However, in the seventeenth and eighteenth centuries only quite literate people (a small minority) would even be aware of the calendar year. Quite often people would know what year of the reign of the current monarch it was, without knowing the calendar year. (Often when asked what year it was, Robert Webbe would reply in terms of years of the monarch's reign, for example, 'Our King George came to the throne in 1714 ... Do you doubt the Royalle Majesties Reign ... ?' See page 67.) This could be one explanation for the discrepancies. As far as his death is concerned, one cannot exclude the possibility that Robert Webbe suffered a stroke, rendering him 'dead' to the outside world, although technically still alive, maybe in a diminished state. If this were true, and he suffered a debilitating stroke in 1733, although not dying until three years later, he would only remember the last year that meant anything to him, which was 1733. Although he thought he died from his legs, it is quite possible that he was actually wrong.

Continuing my research, the facts grew even more confusing, especially when I tried to corroborate the information I found concerning his marriage and children. It appeared that he was wildly wrong, and yet how could he be so inaccurate about his own immediate family? It was now that I first began to suspect that the automatic messages, although apparently originating from one person, were actually coming from two people. I had a statement, signed by 'Robert Webbe', which read,

'My children were Robert, Richard, John, Elizabeth, and Mary. I marryed Mary and my brother marryed Anne. The wife of my poore father passed away and he again married . . .'

In the entries in the marriages section of the Parish Registers I discovered these facts:

'September 26th, 1685, Robert Webb married Penelope Mault.'

'December 17th, 1710, Robert Webb, widower, married Mary Cock.'
'April 6th, 1714, Robert Webb married Anne Willis, widow.'

It was now becoming clear that there *were* two Robert Webbes, presumably father and son. I returned to the baptisms section and found the following entries:

'December 29th, 1714, Robert of Robert and Anne Webb.'
'August 5th, 1716, John of Robert and Anne Webb.'
'October 6th, 1721, Mary of Robert and Anne Webb.'

These entries verified without any shadow of doubt the facts contained in Webbe's automatic writing, except that he had claimed to have had also two other children, Richard and Elizabeth. These exceptions are accounted for by the fact that at some time the Parish Registers were rewritten in part, and not always accurately. There was also the problem that the Rector often only filled in the particulars of baptisms, marriages and burials when a large number had already taken place; this resulted in many entries which should have been recorded being omitted. On top of this, many of the entries which were written down at the time, later fell victim to flood-water, storms, and other acts of God. I believe that in the case of his children Robert Webbe's information was correct; apart from anything else, parents were more likely to have five children than three in the early eighteenth century. The records also confirmed that Robert Webbe did in fact remarry after the death of his first wife.

When I looked through the baptisms section once more to try to discover the names of the children of Robert Webbe senior (the father) I found that he had five children. Four were borne by his first wife, Penelope (Robert, Penelope, Susannah, and James), and one was borne by his second wife, Mary (Mary). Robert Webbe, senior, was buried on August 14th, 1713.

With these newly found facts in mind, I rewrote the original automatic message from 'Robert Webbe' in the form of a double monologue from both of the Robert Webbes. Suddenly it all seemed to make greater sense of a message which otherwise contained a number of factual errors:

R.W. junior: 'My children were Robert, Richard, John, Elizabeth and Mary.' (*Correct*)
R.W. senior: 'I married Mary and my brother (an error for son?) marryed Anne.' (*Correct*)
R.W. junior: 'The wife of my poore father passed away and he again married.' (*Correct*)

As can be seen, in this form all the facts can be verified but in its original form there are totally inexplicable errors.

It did not take very long for me to work out why this strange 'double' communication had occurred. I had never considered that there might have been more than one Robert Webbe and as I had received the majority of the information by mentally asking 'Robert Webbe' to communicate, I had no means of knowing that I was in fact receiving automatic writing from two people who both had the same name, either on different occasions, or together.

I recalled, however, that on previous occasions, although not with Webbe, I had received messages indicating that I was actually transcribing a 'group message'. For example, my grandfather had mentioned in automatic writing a number of times that he was with other deceased relatives and friends as I described in *The Link*. Once he had even requested time to answer a problem I had put to him, so that he might discuss it with others.

Of course this also explained why 'Robert Webbe' had insisted that his father's name was Richard when, according to the contemporary Parish Registers, it was Robert. I was obviously communicating with Robert senior at this point, in which case he might be correct.

\* \* \*

Tracing the immediate family of Robert Webbe senior through contemporary records proved to be rather difficult, especially when it came to finding information about Richard Webbe, the gentleman who was his father according to the automatic writing.

Richard was supposed to have died in 1703, and his wife (Robert senior's mother) Elizabeth, was supposed to have died in 1719. There were no references at all to a Richard Webbe who could fit the dates at which I calculated that he must have been born and married, nor of his burial, allegedly in 1703, in the Linton Parish Registers. I thought that the information contained in the automatic writing really *was* incorrect this time, but as I later discovered, the facts could be verified.

Although there were no references to a Richard Webbe in the Linton Parish Registers, there was a wealth of information to be found concerning him in the Linton Rentall and the Linton Tenements at Will.

The Linton Rentall is a small, hand-written book containing records of everybody who owned or rented property in the village in 1674. In it were a number of references to Mr Richard Webbe:

'Of Mr. Webb for a Shopp in the markett place and one piece of wasteground late within Brands fathers and since the sond. within Brands. £0.3.4
'Of the same for one other shop sometimes Robt. Brands and late John Brands his fathers and since within Brands £0.0.8
Of the same for one other Shop there sometimes Roger Harolds and late the said John Brand. £0.2.0.'

Also held by Mr Webbe at this time, and recorded in the same book, were three more shops in the Market Place, in addition to several acres of farm land around the village, for example,

Of the same for one shot and three whoods of arable land. £0.10.0.'

# The Strangers

'Shot' and 'whood' were, I believe, square measurements of land, similar to acres or hectares.

It was quite clear that, over the years, Mr Webbe had been taking control of a large number of shops until, in the Linton Tenements at will, dated 1678, just four years later than the Rentall, he was described as Richard Webbe, Gent. Generally property would be acquired in the belief that the owner, or indeed tenant, would rise up the social ladder. With the ownership of property came the chance of becoming a 'gentleman', a title which would then be passed from father to eldest son, upon the father's decease. Many of these gentlemen maintained their illusion of 'honours' by purchasing a coat-of-arms to lend further substance to their notions of gentility.

By 1678 a number of entries can be found in the Linton Tenements at Will referring to Richard Webbe; for example,

'Of Richard Webb, Gent. for one Shopp in the Market Place and one piece of wasteground at sometime John Brands and late William Brands.'

This is the same entry as was contained in the Linton Rentalls of 1674. In addition to this property, Richard Webbe now owned another six shops in Linton.

There was no doubt about the existence of Richard Webbe in Linton at the end of the seventeenth century. I was baffled by the fact that someone of such substance in a relatively small village community should apparently go unrecorded in the Parish Registers. It really didn't make sense. But then, almost as if I was being guided, I discovered within the hand-written words inscribed on a large, dried-out roll of vellum the key to the door which had been locked to me. It was contained in a bundle of eighteenth century papers* relating to property transactions in Linton and was a document concerning a house that Richard Webbe had sold to another villager, Robert Flacke, in 1690. (The house, incidentally, was not Queen's House judging by the description given of the building.)

*Kept in the Public Records Office

134

Richard Webbe was described in this document as 'a Grocer of Saffron Walden', and the property which he was selling was actually owned jointly by his wife, named as Hannah.

Obviously I had two new leads in this information, one of which conflicted with something 'Robert Webbe' had written in an automatic message. He had claimed that his mother, and therefore Richard's wife, was called Elizabeth. Hannah was a new name which had not been mentioned before. Saffron Walden was a small market town about five miles from Linton, but just across the Cambridgeshire border in Essex. This was why I had been unable to trace Richard Webbe in the Linton Parish Registers: although he owned a large amount of property in Linton, he was actually domiciled in Saffron Walden, in whose Parish Registers I hoped to find some relevant records of his life and family.

However, far more fascinating, and of much greater importance, were two small, cracked, red wax seals on the bottom edge of this scroll, placed next to the signatures of Richard and Hannah Webbe. It did not take any imagination to see that the seal belonging to Richard was a sheaf of wheat, and that Hannah's seal was a scorpion. This was a really startling piece of evidence, verifying 'Robert Webbe's information. I remembered having been very amused by his pomposity when he told me that he had, as a gentleman, a coat-of-arms.

' 'Tis three shells, two sheaves, a river of Lynton with sheaves and ye family scorpionne.'

He had been telling the truth, contrary to my belief that it was a tale designed to impress. The scorpion and sheaf of wheat embossed in the old red wax were almost identical to his drawing of his family crest.

Why, then, when he was able to give such accurate information about something like this, did his information about his mother seem to contradict the facts as set out in the same document? The simple answer was that he was correct again, as I discovered when I inspected the Saffron Walden Parish Registers. In order to study them, however, I had to make an appointment first with the Vicar of Saffron Walden as the

Parish Registers were still kept in the church. I spent two after-noons in January, 1977, sitting in the vestry of the church, trying to discover more about the enigmatic Richard Webbe, Gent. Although I came away knowing more about him than I did before I started, he was still more of mystery than I would have liked.

Remembering that 'Robert Webbe' had told me that his father had died after falling from his horse in 1703, I turned first to the burial section of the Registers, trying to find record of Richard's burial. I did not find it, and have been unable to trace his death in Parish Registers of Linton, Saffron Walden, or a number of the surrounding smaller villages. This may well be accounted for by the state in which the Saffron Walden Registers had been kept during the late seventeenth and early eighteenth centuries. There are very substantial gaps in the records between 1697 and 1708, including several consecutive years when there were no entries made at all. These years, of course, are among the most important in trying to find a record of Richard's burial. Although I was unable to prove his son's information about the date of his decease, I tend to believe it, not least because of the accuracy of most of his other statements.

Next I tried to trace Richard's birth in the baptisms section, guessing that he was born about 1630–40. It did not take long to find the following entry for the year 1637: 'Richard son of Phillip and Ann Webb, bapt. October 22.'

I then checked, out of curiosity, when Phillip and Ann were married. I discovered that Phillip Webbe married twice; he first married a woman named Ann Cragge on May 10th, 1629, and then, after being widowed, he married Ann Goshing, who also happened to be widowed, on February 21st, 1654.

Phillip Webbe's children, or least those that were recorded, were Ann, born 1635, Edward, born 1642, Mary, born 1645, another Edward, born 1647. Phillip himself died in 1683, by which time he must have been quite an old man.

This information about Phillip and Ann does conflict with the information of 'Robert Webbe' who stated: 'The father of

Richard Webbe was Henry Webbe . . . and his wife Elizabeth.'

I have no explanation for this piece of erroneous information, although contemporary records indicate that Phillip had three brothers, one of whom was called Henry. On a previous occasion Robert Webbe senior had referred to his son as a brother, so he was obviously prone to mistakes, as any human being might be, especially one whose memory may not be very good.

My next piece of research has to be based upon a certain amount of logical guess work because of incomplete records. I next looked for records of Richard's marriage, or marriages, since there were indications that he married twice. I found only one entry in the marriage section, which was dated 1663, and read: 'Richard Webbe married Elizabeth Kinge, 8th June.'

There are no records of any children resulting from that marriage in the Saffron Walden Parish Registers—a result, I am sure, of the lackadaisical way in which the records were kept. However, Robert Webbe senior claimed that his mother was named Elizabeth, his father, as I have said, being Richard. I therefore guess that Robert, senior, was born in the year following this marriage. It was almost certainly by 1665, and I also assume that he was an eldest child as he used the title of 'Gentleman' after his father's death. If he was born in 1664, he would have been aged twenty-one when he married Penelope Mault, and aged twenty-two when his son, Robert, junior, was born in 1686.

There are no records either of the death of Elizabeth Webbe, although Robert Webbe claimed that she died in 1719, which I think is so unlikely as to be incorrect. Unless Richard Webbe left her, or vice versa, which would have been almost unheard of at that time, she died before 1675 because at that date can be found the following entry in the baptisms section of the Parish Registers: 'Thomas Webb son of Mr. Richd. and Hannah, 19th. August.'

By this time, Richard had obviously married Hannah, the wife referred to in the document relating to the sale of a house.

It is also very rare to find anybody referred to as 'Mr' in the Parish Registers. This indicates Richard's position in Saffron Walden, and his substance. There is little doubt that this is the same man referred to as Richard Webbe, Gent., in the Linton Tenements at Will.

That was all I discovered about the enigmatic Richard Webbe, Gent. I have been unable to find any record of his death, and I have been unable to find a record of more than one of his children's baptisms, although I am sure it was not because he had no other offspring.

In a number of places in the automatic scripts, 'Robert Webbe' had mentioned names of people that either he or his family knew. Of course, it is virtually impossible to corroborate such claims, but in one instance he referred to his grandfather's connections with Oliver Cromwell. In fact it was the only occasion on which such name-dropping occurred and after doing some research on Oliver Cromwell, with the assistance of Saffron Walden Museum, I decided that his claim was not entirely outside the bounds of possibility. He had written: 'My grandfather supported the fine Oliver Cromwell and even knewe him at Saffron Walden.'

This information not only indicates that Cromwell had stayed in Saffron Walden, but also that Robert Webbe's grandfather had connections with the town, which he did, as I have just shown. When I approached the Curator of Saffron Walden Museum asking if he knew of any connections that Oliver Cromwell may have had with the town, some interesting information was offered which gave great credence to Webbe's claim.

Oliver Cromwell did indeed have connections with the town during the Civil War. In 1647 while building up a battalion in the area to combat Royalists, he stayed with General Fairfax in a building known as the Sun Inn for twenty-eight days. At this time the Parliamentary Army, of 40,000 men, lay encamped in and around the town. During March, April, and May, conference after conference took place in Saffron

Walden Church between the Commissioners of Parliament and
rank and file 'Deputies', making the church 'nigh full' of those
listening to Government proposals, Fairfax's praises, and
Cromwell's grave speeches.

It would seem highly probable therefore that a gentleman
like Phillip Webbe, who must have been a man of some substance, probably a shopkeeper, would have met Cromwell in
the town at some stage of his stay. The town is so small in any
case that any man as important as Cromwell would not have
gone unseen by anybody. If Phillip Webbe was, for example,
a grocer, as was his son, it is almost inconceivable that Cromwell
could have passed all that time without provisions. Phillip
would have been called upon to supply them.

Having made these various discoveries which corroborated,
or at the least, lent credence to the information of 'Robert
Webbe', I returned to the message from which I had extracted
these facts. It was quite clear now that this message had originated from both senior and junior Robert Webbes; it was actually written at the same time as the previous dual-communica-
tion concerning the wives and children. If read as originating
from one person, it can only be partially correct; rewritten as
a double monologue it is accurate:

| R.W. senior: | 'The name of my mother was Elizabeth.' *(Correct)* |
| R.W. junior: | 'I did knowe of the name of my son and I am most ashamed at such a deed when I set my eyes upon it.' (Referring to J. Webbe's name inscribed on a brick on an outside wall.) |
| R.W. senior: | 'My grandfather supported the fine Oliver Cromwell and even knewe him at Saffron Walden.' |

The reference to Cromwell must have been made by
Robert senior because if it was made by Robert junior Richard
Webbe, his grandfather, would have been only ten years old
at the time of Cromwell's stay. Robert senior's grandfather,

Phillip, would have been contemporary with Cromwell, who was born in 1599.

It is possible to gain an insight into the Civil War and Linton's involvement with it by reading one or two entries in the Linton Parish Registers of that time. Under the date of June 16th, 1648, are the following entries:

'John Sendall, of Brinckley, gent., slaine in a skirmish by the Parliament forces, was buried.
'Robert Giles, of Newport, slaine at the same time and upon the same occasion, was buried.
'A stranger at the same time slaine, was buried.'

These are the only records in our village Registers of any deaths resulting from the Civil War, perhaps because the area was inhabited largely by staunch supporters of Cromwell, who was a local man. This doubtless explains why Robert Webbe regarded Cromwell as a 'fine man'. However, I digress.

Having now checked all the information regarding his family that Robert Webbe had given in the automatic writing, and having been able to corroborate the great majority of it, I turned my attention to the other facts that he had included in his scripts. I remembered that I was now dealing with two men rather than one, and that between them they spanned a period of over seventy years, from 1664 to 1736. Of course, the easiest information to verify was that which included names which could in theory be quickly traced in the Parish Registers, as I had already done with Webbe's own family.

The name which had appeared most frequently throughout the automatic messages was that of 'my goode man Robert Moore', from whom Webbe claimed to buy provisions, as he described them. One of the four tradesmen's tokens in my father's possession had apparently been issued by this gentleman, in 1667.

Contained within the pages of the Parish Registers were a considerable number of entries for the Moore family; however, the only reference to Robert Moore that I could find here was in the burial section, and once again it verified more of Webbe's information. It read: 'Robert Moore, Grocer, buried, May 20th., 1713.'

Robert Moore was a grocer, just as I had been told. But the fact that he died in 1713, the same year as Robert Webbe senior, suggested that the messages referring to him could only have been made by Robert senior. I remembered one occasion when I had been informed: 'And so off with goode wyfe to see my goode man Rob: Moore and a fine lunch two.'

Robert Webbe junior from whom I believed these messages to be originating, was unlikely to have been a close friend of a man who was not his comtemporary. Moore was with little doubt a friend of Robert senior which surely makes sense as Robert's father was himself a grocer; also both men were important figures in Linton at this time and their friendship undoubtedly sprang from business associations. Then I recalled the occasion when my father's tokens had vanished. When questioned about this, 'Robert Webbe' had answered: 'I must use such tokens as you cannot spend them. If I see them I can use them to pay my provisions for my goode man Robert Moore.'

It had puzzled my father at the time that Robert Webbe, whom we believed to have lived from 1678 to 1733, should want to 'use' the tokens. According to Robert junior he would have been born nine years *after* the date on Robert Moore's token; (in fact he was born nineteen years after the token was circulated). These tradesmen's tokens were rarely in use for more than five years, certainly never more than fifteen years at the very most; in their very nature they were only temporary as they were issued in lieu of small change at times when there were shortages of small denomination coins. Why should the Robert Webbe whom we believed to be responsible for the automatic writing wish to take something which could have been of no use to him?

They could, though, be used by Robert, senior, although the tokens must have been close to the end of their useful life even for himself. If Robert senior was born in 1664, he would have been only three when Moore first issued his token. Assuming that the Linton tokens stayed in circulation for between ten and fifteen years, Robert senior would have had use for them as a young man. In fact, all four of the tradesmen who issued tokens were contemporaries of Robert senior rather than his son, which helps to identify the origin of many of the automatic scripts.

On another occasion, Webbe had referred to someone called Daniel Bittin, writing: 'Indeede I even knowe of one Daniel Bittin of Lynton.'

There is only one Daniel Bittin recorded anywhere in the Linton Parish Registers, and he was baptised on January 22nd, 1648. This certainly makes him a contemporary of Robert senior as he would have been thirty-eight at the time of Robert junior's birth in 1686. In the same Daniel Bittin message, a gentleman named Matthew Hunter was mentioned: 'Indeede I once knewe of one Matthew Hunter of this same village.'

In this particular case I was able to prove that Robert Webbe most certainly knew Matthew Hunter. I happened to find on a page in the Parish Registers a hand-written memorandum; it consisted of a list of names headed, 'Excom.', meaning excommunicated. The names are:

| | |
|---|---|
| Edward Smith | Matthew Hunter and his wife |
| Robert Stubbin | Robert Webb and his wife |
| Widow Brown, sen. | William Page and his wife |
| William Cowle | The wife of John Clarke |
| William Stinton | John Partridg. |

No reason is given in the Parish Registers for their excommunication and there is no note to explain the list. I did discover, however, that at the Quarter Sessions held in Cambridge on January 13th, 1675, several Linton inhabitants were convicted of nonconformity, amongst them being Edward Smith, husbandman, William Page, widow Unnyer, Robert Stubbin and his wife. The penalty for this offence was £20 a month for as long as the convicted person failed to attend Holy Communion. This particular list does not include Robert Webbe and his wife for the obvious reason that they were not married until ten years later. The memorandum in the Parish Registers therefore must have been made after 1685. However, this list showed that Robert Webbe, senior, and Matthew Hunter were 'partners in crime'.

During the course of communicating with 'Robert Webbe', he had referred to several tradesmen in Cambridge from whom he claimed to buy goods. The names of two of these men were Daniel Hardwick and Oliver Camperon.

'... must to my glover Daniel Hardwicke ... in Cambridge,'
and,
'Also to see mine man Oliver Camperon.'

I perused the Parish Registers of a number of churches in Cambridge; there were indeed references in the Registers of the Parish of St Edwards to a family named Hardwick. However, the records were once again badly kept and incomplete and I found no record of Daniel Hardwick. Interestingly, I could not find any references to a family by the name of Camperon, although I was able to find a number of records relating to a family called CAMPION. It is not unlikely that there were deviations in the spelling of the same name, or more likely that Robert Webbe was unable to spell their name correctly.

A good example of how the same surname was spelled in various differing forms came to light when I researched another of Webbe's statements: '... ye stupidde James Onyon my footman and servant.'

I was unable to find a record of a James Onyon in the Linton Parish Registers, but I did find a number of men with the same name recorded in various sections of the Saffron Walden Parish Registers. The name Onyon was spelled in various ways, including, Onion, Unnyer, Union, Unyer, and Onnyer. I also checked through the Linton Tenements at Will, the Linton Rentall, and other documents relating to the holding of property and found no references to the Onyons, indicating that they held no land. They were probably therefore labourers or working people. It is very likely for this reason that an Onyon would have been a servant for a gentleman of the village.

I was surprised at the various permutations of the spelling of the Webbe's own name; they included, Web, Webb, Webbe, Weeb, and Weebe. In automatic writing, the name was always spelt WEBBE, which is the form I have used in this book, unless I am quoting directly from contemporary documents in which case I have reproduced it as I have found it written.

The name 'Barnarde' was another that I tried to find in the Linton Parish Registers as Webbe had so frequently referred to 'blessed Barnarde' in disparaging terms. This person certainly existed, as Barnarde was the name of one of Linton's largest families in the eighteenth century.

At one time Robert Webbe had told me in automatic writing that he believed his family to have originated from the neighbouring village of Bartlow, about a mile and a half from Linton, and about five miles from Saffron Walden, around 1565. I found a number of references in the Linton Parish Registers, and also in the Rent Roll of Linton Manor in 1560 which lent great substance to this claim. Not only were there no references to the Webbe family in the Parish Registers before 1563, but two entries in the baptisms section referred to a family named Webbe 'of Bartlow'.

A 'Jo. Web' was baptised on August 10th, 1566, and his father, also Jo. Web of Bartlow had married Hellon Hockley in 1564. This John Webbe was mentioned in the Rent Roll of Linton Manor of 1560:

'John Webb of Bartlowe lykwise holdeth one Tenement with a Close adjoyning called Burstelors.'

I think that this information speaks for itself, and again corroborates Webbe's facts.

On two occasions Robert Webbe had mentioned specific names of streets in Linton during the eighteenth century, neither of which exists in the twentieth century. The first was 'Butchers Rowe', the second, 'Hoggs Lane'. He claimed that his business premises were in Butchers Rowe, and that his father, Richard, had been killed in Hoggs Lane in 1703. It was not at all easy to trace either of these names, and in fact I could not find any written evidence of Hoggs Lane. However, anybody studying a map of Linton dated 1620, which is the only map of the village made until enclosure in about 1845, will immediately realize just how difficult it is to trace individual tracks and lanes. Only the main streets are actually named, for example, the High Streete, Cambridge Roade, the Hadstocke Roade, etc. There are many smaller roadways and lanes which must have been named by the villagers but which are now unrecorded. Hoggs Lane is, I am sure, an example. Butchers Rowe did not prove easy to trace, and again I was unable to find it marked on the map of 1620, but I did find reference to it in some of the Linton Rent Rolls. It was a row of shops leading off from the Market Place, which reminded me of the entries in the Linton Rentalls and other documents referring to property owned by Richard Webbe 'in the Markette Place'.

I have been unable to discover what the Robert Webbes sold in their many shops from original records, although Robert Webbe, senior, claimed to have been a 'trader of grain', or what is now known as a corn merchant. Both Robert Webbes are referred to in original records as 'Gentleman', which in fact is how both referred to themselves in their automatic writings. 'I am Rob:Webbe,Gent.', they would write.

As there are records of other members of the Webbe family having been farmers, it is very possible that the Robert Webbes, both senior and junior, were corn merchants, or vendors of farm produce. In the Parish Registers is an entry in the burial section concerning a John Webbe, farmer, who died in 1663. Also Millicent Webbe, to whom I return later, said that her father, Henry, was a farmer.

Having now researched most of the information supplied by the Robert Webbes, as I now knew 'Robert Webbe' to be, I proceeded to investigate some of the other material which I had collected since 1971. There were a number of other points to consider and to research, especially if I was going to try to substantiate my theory about there having been two Robert Webbes. Which of the two gentlemen had I seen on the staircase and in my parents' bedroom? Who was responsible for the writing on the wall, and who had been responsible for the trail of apported objects left around the house? From which of the two Webbes did the strange smells originate? These now became issues that were as important as the facts contained in the automatic scripts.

Before I begin to expound my ideas on these various phenomena, and before I make any attributions, I think that I should describe briefly the plan of the house, and the way in which it has been built and extended over the years, because the dates at which various parts of the house were built are directly relevant if one is going to try to distinguish between the two Webbes.

The first part of the house to be built was a standard three-roomed, timber-framed structure, a typical East Anglian house. It is not known who built this house, but it must have been constructed during the first quarter of the seventeenth century. A building is shown on the site of Queen's House on the map of Linton dated 1620, owned by someone called Thomas Salmon; whether this is the same house that still stands is unknown. The house is of standard dimensions which are common to all houses of the same age, being one 'bay' wide, a bay being approximately sixteen feet. This section of the house has oak mullioned windows with leaded glass panels.

To this three-roomed building was added at some time in the mid-seventeenth century a brick structure, also with oak mullioned windows. It was this house which Robert Webbe senior knew. Robert junior was undoubtedly raised in this building, and was more than likely born in it in 1686. Robert senior died eighteen years before his son added the main front to the house in 1731. This part of the house was built of locally made red bricks; there were pine-wood window sashes, and the interior was panelled throughout with pine.

The original building, however, almost certainly consisted

of one groundfloor room and a first floor room of exactly the same dimensions above it; the two were connected by a ladder through a hole in the floor, as was standard practice in houses of this time. The third room was probably more of a hall which was used for storage purposes, or even for keeping animals in. It may, however, have been used as another room and put to ordinary domestic use. It was this room, known and used by Robert senior that Robert junior chose to use to accommodate the ornately carved pine staircase which he had built when the front of his house was constructed. Both Robert Webbes were therefore aware of this area of the house whilst they were alive, although each put it to different use. (See diagram pages 6 and 7.)

Bearing in mind the dates at which various sections of the house had been built, I returned to the material I had relating to the person I had seen in the house. I came to the conclusion that the apparition that I had seen and experienced was that of Robert junior (1686–1736). I based this conclusion on two issues which, in my opinion, prove that the ghost I actually saw was the son.

First of all, I had seen him either on the staircase, or in my parents' bedroom. Both of these two areas are contemporary with Robert junior. In fact, neither existed during the lifetime of Robert senior. I consider that this is evidence that the son was the gentleman still walking in his part of the house.

Secondly, I considered the costume worn by the apparition. Consulting one of the definitive works on the history of English costumes (*A Handbook of English Costume in the Eighteenth Century* by C. Willett Cunnington and Phillis Cunnington), I found that the clothes worn by Robert Webbe, as I had noted them at the time, were fashionable between about 1730 and 1740.

He had been wearing a frock coat embroidered around the edges; it displayed large buttons down the front, and also large, embroidered cuffs. It appeared to be collarless. All these details were fashionable between about 1710 to 1740, but what really dated the costume more precisely were the cuffs and pockets of Webbe's coat. Cuffs were fairly wide until 1710, when they narrowed with the sleeve; the size varied but the depth was moderate until about 1727.

'In the 1730s the cuff was very deep, spreading upwards; the cuff wings curved round the back of the elbow and the decorative buttons were often placed above the bend of the elbow,' says *A Handbook of English Costume in the Eighteenth Century*.

This description tallies exactly with the cuff that I saw on Webbe's coat, and which I included on my sketch made at the time I first saw him, and on my subsequent more detailed drawing.

The same book also describes pockets as having straight-bordered flaps, until 1710. After this time, the borders became scalloped. The pocket I observed on the coat did not have a straight edge; it dipped down into a single scallop. The pocket was also positioned at waist level, which is indicative that the coat was made after 1720 as, before this time, the pockets were somewhat lower.

The full-bottomed wig worn by Robert Webbe was in common with what was in fashion until the early 1730s; after that date it was still worn by older men.

These facts all lead me to believe that the apparition was that of Robert Webbe junior. The clothes that he was wearing would not have been worn during his father's lifetime.

Having proved this, I returned to the automatic writings which referred to Webbe's 'bad legs'. Then I became temporarily confused because I found in one message: 'Try and comfort my poore wife Mary who weeps every morning in my bedchamber as my legs rotte before oure eyes'.

Mary was the wife of Robert senior. And yet the ghost that I had seen on the staircase had complained of his legs, and was supporting himself on two sticks, as he was when I again saw him in the bedroom. It was also in this bedroom that my father had undergone the unpleasant experience with his legs in the middle of the night. Robert senior can have had no connections with this room, and would not have known the staircase built by his son.

There is a good explanation for this anomolous situation. The symptoms felt by my father in the toes and legs during the unpleasant nocturnal experiences, when he heard another man's stubbly chin rubbing against the sheets and heard somebody else breathing heavily beside him, were those of gout. It will also be recalled that Thomas Penn had claimed that Robert Webbe died from gout. It is a disease prompted by lack of hygiene, an excessive consumption of fermented liquor, too much rich food, and too little exercise. I am certain that all of these conditions were applicable to both of the Robert Webbes.

However, according to medical sources, gout, as well as being the result of these things, is also a hereditary disease frequently passed from father to son. This also confirms what Thomas Penn claimed.

I think the evidence is overwhelming: both father and son contracted the disease, and I feel sure that it claimed the life of the elder Robert Webbe, and probably that of the younger one too. As I have already suggested, it is possible that the son, although having gout, and believing that this was the cause of his demise, actually suffered a debilitating coronary in the latter years of his life. It is a pity that medical records do not exist.

It is not so easy to attribute the writing on the wall to either of the Webbes, and I tend to think that it was the joint work of both of them. It all seems to make sense in retrospect, but at the time we could not understand why Robert Webbe had signed his name twice, when nowhere else was a signature repeated. Obviously, it was because there were two Robert Webbes communicating; each signed his name on the wall.

As far as this particular phenomenon is concerned, I do not believe that each name on the wall was signed by the 'spirit' of the person to whom it belonged. What makes more sense is that Robert Webbe, or the Webbes, wrote the majority of the signatures themselves which accounts for the fact that many are inscribed in the same handwriting. However, a certain number of the signatures are not in the handwriting associated with the Webbes, and are obviously signatures 'written', or somehow transmitted or transcribed, of the people they claim to represent.

If the dates supplied with the names are recorded in different chronological tables, it will be found that a majority are dates that are contemporary with Robert senior, rather than Robert junior. There are of course many dates which are contemporary with neither of the two men, which indicates that we know too little of the mechanics of communication after death. When the names had been completed, 'Robert Webbe' had written: 'I have now finished my worke although methinks I can indever to fynd some more names soon ... and I must go to see my good man Robert Moore ...'

This reference to Moore suggests that Robert Webbe senior was the instigator of the graffiti phenomenon. For what reason he chose a wall in a room which was not in existence during his lifetime on which to execute his desire to help me, I am not sure. The same apparent lack of logic can be applied to the removal of the tradesmen's tokens kept in the sitting room, another part of the house unknown to Robert senior. I think that our notions of hauntings should perhaps be looked at again. Whose standards of logic should be applied in judging such cases?

It should also be remembered that there are many, many records of 'crisis apparitions' that have appeared in places very far from where they have their normal existence. A parent, for example, may be in Australia at the time of an accident involving an offspring in England. This may create what is termed a 'crisis apparition' when the child, and the outline of its predicament will appear to the parent in Australia, where the child has never been. In his book, *Apparitions*, G. N. M. Tyrrell describes such cases.

I believe therefore that it is not beyond the scope of apparitions like Robert Webbe senior to instigate writing on a wall of whose existence he would have been unaware whilst alive, or for him to remove tokens from a room in a building not in existence during his lifetime.

Something which had always puzzled people when told

about the writing on the wall was the fact that Robert Webbe used a pencil to make the inscriptions. Even though I left two pencils which were periodically sharpened on the bed, how would he know what a pencil was? It seems to be a common impression that the only writing implements used before the beginning of the twentieth century were quills. This is not so. Pencils have been in existence since the end of the sixteenth century, since the German scientist, Konrad Gesner, became the first man to put graphite in wood to make a pencil, in 1565. It was the first serious rival to the quill. Robert Webbe would therefore have known what a pencil was, and for what it was used.

I think it is impossible to attribute the origin of any of the strange smells, the piped tobacco smoke, the old books, the bad breath, or the spicy smells, to either of the Webbes. However, it has been noticed that many of the smells, more especially an unpleasant odour like rotting cabbage, appear when a stranger enters the house for the first time through the front door. This, and the fact that most of the smells are noticed in the front of the house, associated with Robert Webbe junior suggest that he was responsible for these phenomena. On one occasion when there was a reek of pipe tobacco smoke in my parents' bedroom, Robert Webbe had 'claimed responsibility', saying that he did 'fancey a wholesome pipe of tobacco'. From which of the Webbes this originated, is open to conjecture.

I think it would be tedious for the reader if I was to list again *all* the automatic writings that I received from 'Robert Webbe', giving my reasons for believing that they originate from either the elder or junior Robert Webbe. Quite apart from any other consideration, I think that it is not an easy job to distinguish in many cases whether the messages originated from father or son. I shall, however, expound my thoughts on some of the more interesting scripts from the Robert Webbes.

I am of the opinion that of the two men the father was a more passive person, interested only in his family, his friends, and his business. He seems not to have had any great attachment to any part of the house, maybe because he was not responsible for having built any of it. Robert Webbe, junior, was far more bombastic and pompous, living from the fruits of success cultivated by his father and grandfather. It was he who lived to excess, was totally materialistic and, according to contemporary records, although he makes no reference to it himself, lost all the family's assets and money. (*His* son, Robert, was a 'glazier and plumber', who died in 1756.) It was Robert junior who built the front of the house, who became obsessed with the fact that he owned it, and who remained in it decades after he had died.

'Robert Webbe' described on one occasion objects and furnishings in the house which belonged to us; two items which he said he liked were: '... ye delicate art such as ye picture of my Lady in the front room ... The handles of the new chest in myne room did tincle as I layed on the bed ...'

Both of these items were kept in the front of the house, Robert junior's 'territory'; the portrait to which he referred hangs in the sitting room and the chest with brass handles that rattle against their back plates is kept in my parents' bedroom.

It must have been Robert junior who claimed that the house 'is myne house and myne all', because in the same automatic message, and without a break where the father might 'slip in', he referred to 'the shiney gold candle holder in my staires'. This particular light fitting hangs above the staircase that Robert junior built. The father would not have described the room as having any connections with a staircase because as far as *he* was concerned, it was an empty room. 'Robert Webbe' also admitted having placed a candle in our cloakroom, although he referred to the same room as a 'servery'. Again, this room was not in existence at the time of the father's life.

When two framed prints disappeared from my parents' bedroom, 'Robert Webbe' said that they could be found in his 'secrette hole'. This aperture is in Robert junior's part of the house; when told that my father was angry at their 'theft', Webbe retorted: 'This house is myne and I owne all of ye same.'

Just as Robert junior was responsible for the disappearance

of our belongings, so was he responsible for the introduction
into the house of other people's belongings, or apports. Every
such object has been discovered in the front of the house, that
part of the building associated with him.

The menus were the work of Robert senior I am sure. Firstly,
whenever food was mentioned to 'Robert Webbe', a reference
was made to 'my goode man Robert Moore', whom, as I have
already explained, was a contemporary of the father. Secondly,
on the occasion that a menu was written completely automatically by 'Robert Webbe', the envelope onto which it was inscribed had been left in the kitchen, a room in the back of the
house which was the father's territory.

The fact that it appears to have been the father who was
interested in food and in cooking, indicates again that he was
more refined and, in a rustic manner, more cultured than his
boorish son. It is interesting that even when I received the
messages from 'Robert Webbe', I noticed that 'he' always
showed deference to tradesmen, or anybody on whom 'he'
depended for anything. In fact I am now of the opinion that
Robert senior being a milder, more refined man was always
polite and deferential to others; it was his son who was not.
Other people, in the eyes of Robert junior, were merely men
with whom to trade (and I expect swindle, given a chance),
or they were 'bumpkins'.

I had been called a bumpkin when I tried to tell Robert
junior that it was not 1727, but 1972.

When Robert Webbe was convinced that it was May 29th,
1728, he had told me that he was visiting in Cambridge two
men: '... must to my glover Daniel Hardwicke ...', and, '...
also to see mine man Oliver Camperon'. Joining Webbe on his
journey was, '... ye stupidde James Onyon my footman.'

Robert Webbe senior would have referred to the tradesmen
as 'goode' men. Robert junior always referred to tradesmen as
'his' men, as if trying to give the impression that he owned them
in some way. This, of course, is in character with his desire to
impress others with his ownership of material possessions. One
also is struck by the vanity of Robert junior in many of his

messages: '... some snuff for my delicate nose ...', and, '... to see the goodes that catch mine pretty eyes.'

But perhaps I am too hard on Robert junior. Maybe he was a typical gentleman of his time, and his father was the soft-mannered exception.

Millicent Webbe was never so much of a 'person' to our family as 'Robert Webbe' had been, partly, I suppose, because she had been a more traditional ghost—the sort of ghost that passes in the night. Her 'life' as far as we were concerned, and as far as she had been concerned, was not very long. Strangely enough, her information through automatic writing appeared at the time to be more feasible and more cogent than that of 'Robert Webbe', but it proved far more difficult to substantiate through contemporary documents, chiefly because her facts related to an earlier, and therefore darker, period of documentary evidence.

'I am Millicent born here 1655,' she had written. And, 'Ruth and Henry Webbe', were her parents.

An entry in the baptisms section of the Linton Parish Registers in the year 1655 reads: 'Millicent of Ruth and Henry Webb, November 20.'

She had informed me that she died at the age of fifteen in 1670, after giving birth to a child who was apparently illegitimate. I found no record of her burial in the Linton Parish Registers, nor any record of a burial of what would have been described as 'a base childe', had her young baby, which she had killed at birth, been buried. In case her information was incorrect, or in case she was spinning an elaborate story, I also checked for her name in the marriage section of the Parish Registers; I also sought her name in the burials section from the year 1655 to 1745; there are no further references to her. Of course, if it was known that she had indeed taken the life of her child and had died shortly afterwards herself, she would not have been buried in consecrated ground, as she would have been regarded as a murderess in the seventeenth century. This is why her name fails to appear in the burial section of the Parish

Registers, in my opinion. No doubt her baby would have been buried with her at the same time, also escaping entry in the Registers.

This is also a very salient reason for her being unhappy even in death. She thought, probably correctly, that her family and the village were shunning her for her terrible crimes, first that of conceiving an illegitimate child, and second, that of murdering it. She merely wanted forgiveness: 'Pray to God... Forgive me my sins ... I cannot forever suffer ...', she had pleaded.

Millicent had also referred to the children of her uncle Richard, father of Robert senior. As I have already explained, Richard Webbe of Saffron Walden is an enigma as far as records go; only one child of his is recorded, Thomas, born in 1675. Curiously, Millicent refers only to, 'Little Richard, John, and Sarah'. Obviously if she died in 1670 she would have been unaware of Thomas. But she does not mention Robert who would have been about six years old in 1670. Maybe her list of his children is incomplete and perhaps she did not know Richard's family so closely if they lived in another town.

She had also said that 'Richard is brother of Henry all of one house'. She also explained that the two brothers shared the house, although by 1690 Richard was living in Saffron Walden according to records. It is my guess that they shared the house until Richard moved away, perhaps to be nearer to his main shop in Saffron Walden. I do not know the date of his departure, but he was married in Saffron Walden in 1663 which suggests that he lived there by then, or at least had stronger connections with that town than with Linton. Maybe his first wife came from Saffron Walden which is why they married there. However, I think it likely that Richard inherited the house in its entirety from his brother upon the latter's decease. From then it was passed to Richard's eldest son, Robert senior, perhaps without Richard ever moving back into it again. For all anybody knows, Henry may have left it to Robert senior and not his brother. There is no way of telling what happened as there are no documents in existence now which might throw light on the matter, and no will has survived of Henry Webbe. Furthermore, the deeds in our possession relating to the house date back only to 1877.

Henry Webbe's signature is inscribed on the study wall but instead of it being just a name and a date as most of them are, it reads: 'Henry Webbe 1678. My house.'

During the seventeenth century householders were required to pay a tax on each hearth, if there were more than four hearths in the house. In 1674 Henry Webbe paid tax on seven hearths, which happens to be the number there would have been in Queen's House at that time. These two facts prove that the ownership of the house was with Henry at least until 1678. However, if Robert junior was born in the house as he claimed, Henry must have died by 1686.

I am surprised that these two brothers, Henry and Richard, are so little recorded, since they were both reasonably important figures, especially Richard.

Millicent had written that her brothers were called, Henry, John, Phillip, Thomas and James; her sisters, she told me, were Ruth, Katherine and Rachel. Although I found it strange that I could find no reference to them in the Parish Registers of Linton, I did find numerous mentions of their names on other documents relating to the village, which indicated that they did exist, even if their baptisms, marriages, and burials were unrecorded.

I had presumed that Thomas, 'who live in the churchyarde', had died in infancy but this does not appear to be the case. Evidently he merely died before Millicent which is why she refers to him in this euphemistic manner. His name appears on the Linton Rent Rolls of 1654 when he rented a 'glovers stall in the market place' from Lawrence Dockril for 8 shillings per annum. This was however the only reference to him that I found.

I found a number of references to Phillip. In the University Library in Cambridge is a copy of his will, dated 1704, in which he is described as a 'cordwainer'. However, as Millicent had claimed, the Linton Land Assessement of 1694 described him as a shoemaker.

John Webbe is recorded in the Linton Tenements at Will of 1678 as owning, 'a field forward of Lynton wood'.

He also appears in the Linton Land Assessment of 1704, paying rates on an undescribed piece of land, as well as on land described as being 'late Webb's', which presumably had belonged to his father.

However, the most fascinating reference I discovered relating to any of the children was concerned with Millicent's elder sister Katherine Webbe in the Linton Rent Roll of 1654.

'Of Katherine Webb for one piece of a messuage and waste-ground thereunto annexed late John Jordans her grandfather. £0.8.0.'

Millicent had already described her grandfather as 'grandfather Jordan', and her mother's maiden name was Jordan. It would seem that this piece of ground on which Katherine paid 'rates' was a legacy left to her by her grandfather, or left in trust to her. According to Millicent's facts though, her sister was nineteen years old in 1670, which means she would have been only about three years old when she paid rates on the land. Are Millicent's facts incorrect, or was the ground left as a gift in trust upon Mr Jordan's death? I am not sure, but I tend to believe that my latter theory is probably the most likely.

Henry Webbe, according to Millicent, was born in 1620 and died in 1679; her mother lived from 1623 to 1679. Henry Webbe was baptised on October 4th, 1625, and there is no record of his burial; I found no record of the baptism of Ruth Jordan, her mother, although she was buried on April 13th, 1684. I am not sure how Millicent knew at what date her parents died as they both outlived her anyway; I do not consider that she was wildly incorrect in the date of her father's birth. One also should remember that I was asking for dates of birth and the Parish Registers only record the date of *baptism*.

I had on one occasion asked Millicent who the brothers and

sisters of her father had married. Her reply was, 'Richard and Hannah', 'Will. and Lettice', and, 'Ann and Barnabas Paye'.

Richard and Hannah are already known; William Webbe married Lettice Burling in 1641, and Ann Webbe married Barnabas Page (not Paye) in 1662, according to Parish Registers.

Despite considerable research, these are the only facts that I have been able to corroborate, or ascertain any information about. Most of the children to whom she refers are, as far as I can deduce, unrecorded in the Parish Registers. This does not of course mean that her information is incorrect, or that these people did not exist.

The information that I have managed to check certainly appears to be quite accurate; there is little to choose between the 'direct hits' scored with the information of the two Robert Webbes, and that of Millicent. A greater proportion of the Roberts' information can be verified, however.

I have reported in these pages the facts as they were recorded at the time that 'Robert Webbe' was alive; as can be seen, many facts passed unrecorded or have been subsequently the victims of time. It seemed at first that I faced a dilemma because it was apparent that at least half of 'Robert Webbe's' information was quite incorrect; I was unsure about how to reconcile facts that could be verified with facts that were disproved by contemporary records and documents. Having solved one dilemma with the realization that there were two gentlemen by the same name, I then faced another. Should I alter the original manuscript of this book, or should I leave it as it was? I decided that it was far better for the reader to be under the impression that there was only one Robert Webbe (1678–1733) than to know all along that there was a father and a son. This also means that the reader can share the same feelings that I experienced when I discovered that there were two Robert Webbes.

Of course, in retrospect it was all so obvious. At times it seems that they were almost at their wits' end trying to make me aware that there were really two of them. Two of the first three names to be inscribed on the wall were both 'Rob:Webbe'; this is the only name to have been repeated more than once. Certain discrepancies in dates given in the automatic writing were simply ignored by us although they were obvious pointers that the messages must have originated from two different sources.

I am also aware that having explained a number of discrepancies that were in the original text, I have exposed other discrepancies at the same time. However, these discrepancies only remain because of our limited knowledge of the mechanics and causes of psychic phenomena, especially in the field of apparitions which have been the victims of dark churchyards and headless coachmen for decades. I hope that this record serves to dispel some of the popular myths commonly associated with 'ghost stories'. I feel that the story of 'Robert Webbe' is more than just a ghost story; apart from anything else it is one of the few cases where an apparition has been identified, and it is also, to the best of my knowledge, one of the few cases in which extended communication has occurred with an apparition.

Although experiences of the type I have described in this book do not generally interest the scientific community amongst whom I have worked for a number of years, I hope that they will not dismiss them entirely. I should like to hope that this book will serve to broaden our horizons a little and to push us towards reconsidering our views of life, death, and time.

The final judgement is with the reader who may find it believable, partially believable, or totally unbelievable.

What do you think?

# Appendix 2: The Names Inscribed on the Study Walls

After completing my research in the Cambridgeshire County Records Office on all Robert Webbe's information, I decided to try to trace as many as possible of the names which had been inscribed on the walls of the study in 1971. Did these people really exist? What was the relevance of the date under each signature? Did the people whose names appeared on the walls have any connections with the house, Robert Webbe, or the Webbe family in general, I wondered?

I made an alphabetical list of all the names, and began checking each one against the index of the typewritten transcripts of the Linton parish registers. I quickly realized, however, that I had set myself a formidable task if I was really to check each name individually. For example, in order to trace 'John Crane 1733', I had to find his family name in the index. Listed after 'Crane' were about fifty numbers of pages on which could be found a record of a member of the Crane family. To trace any one name could take up to twenty minutes and I realized that with over 500 names to research, several months work was involved. Of course some names, usually those belonging to members of smaller families, were relatively quick and easy to find.

For this reason, although I have positively identified a large number of the names which I consider a representative cross-section, I have not necessarily traced *each* name individually. I have attempted to trace the *family* of each name where possible. Therefore in the following list of the names and dates on the walls, I have marked a number of them with an asterisk which denotes that although a family of that name existed in the village, I have not specifically traced that particular member of it. Names followed by a question mark are those of which I have been unable to find any record. I also discovered on occasions that a name was written on the wall with a date which did not coincide with the dates at which the family were known to have lived in Linton, according to Parish Registers. For example, on the wall is inscribed 'Henry Banks 1858'; according to Registers, however, no such family lived in the village at that particular period. Four references can be found relating to a family with this surname living in Linton between 1633 and 1685. In these instances I have marked the name with an asterisk, but have placed the dates 1633–85 after it.

After I had attempted to trace as many as possible of the names through the Linton Parish Registers, I searched the records kept by other parishes in the area, attempting to identify some of the names not recorded in the Linton Registers.

This proved successful. After all, Robert Webbe had never indicated that the names always belonged to people who lived in Linton. Therefore, after each name I have written the name of the village to which I have traced the family or name. Although I have searched the Parish Registers of Linton, West Wratting, West Wickham, Weston Colville, Carlton, Gt Abington, Hildersham, Bartlow, Gt Shelford, and Cambridge (St Edward's), I have not exhausted all the available registers. There are many other small villages in the surrounding area such as Balsham, Babraham, and Horseheath; there are also many villages in the counties bordering Cambridgeshire in the Linton area. To trace inhabitants of villages in other counties— like Essex, Suffolk, and Hertfordshire—would entail considerable travel and further research. I am fairly certain that probably most of the people whose names are written on the walls did exist.

Several names appear to be of Flemish or continental origin; for example, de Buvais, Dupont, and Oubonet; I believe that such people, although not recorded in our Parish Registers, could well have been living in the area at the time suggested by the date accompanying the name. Linton is on an inland route from east coast ports like Harwich from which foreign merchants travelled. There was also an influx of engineers from the Low Countries during the eighteenth century who came to build canals and dykes in the fens around Cambridgeshire.

In the Parish Registers of a neighbouring village, Gt Abington, I found a memorandum:

'1711. On Thursday June 7th. in the afternoon a ball of fire about a foot in diameter fell with an extraordinary clap of thunder in the lower yard of Mr. Western's house into a pool of water.'

This is a record of either ball-lightning or a meteorite falling to earth. At the time this memorandum was written, neither was scientifically accepted. It seemed ironic that I should find this record of a phenomenon which is now scientific fact whilst researching something which commands the same degree of controversy today that meteorites and ball-lightning commanded two centuries ago.

A

Sarah Ackers 1742 (There is no trace in the Linton Parish Registers of a family by this name. However, Henry Webb married Ann Accow, alias Acker, 31st October, 1780.)

Henrietta Adcock 1701 (*Linton)

John Adcock 1782 (*Linton)

Edward Allern 1822 (*Linton)

Dorothy Alyngton 1677 (Miss Dorothie Dalton of West Wratting (b. November 28, 1605), married Sir Giles Alyngton of Horseheath, December 2nd, 1630. According to a family memorial in Horseheath church, Sir Giles and Lady Dorothy had ten children, including a daughter, also named Dorothy. Lady Dorothy Alyngton died

of smallpox in 1644 which suggests that the signature on the wall is that of her daughter.)

Sarah Armstrong 1651 (?)

Charles Ashbey 1656 (*Linton)

William Asbye 1556 (*Linton)

B

Richard Baines 1772 (*Linton)

Horace Baker 1697 (*Linton)

Robert Baker 1777 (*Linton)

Emma Baldwin 1733 (*Linton)

John Baldwin 1729 (This gentleman married Mary Webb, May 30th, 1730, *Linton.)

Henry Banks 1858 (*Linton 1633-85)

Roger ye Barber 1495 (*Linton)

Jane Barclay 1727 (?)

Richard Barclay 1733 (?)

Richard Barclay (?)

Nathaniel Barham (?)

Elizabeth Barnarde 1800 (*Linton)

Millicent Barnarde 1727 (*Linton)

Richard Barnarde 1735 (This gentleman married Elizabeth Webb in 1732, *Linton.)

Elizabeth Barre 1666 (?)

Rich: Barre 1710 (?)

Charles Bateson 1771, Sophie Bateson 1810 (There is no record of a family by this name, although a family called BATSON lived in the area at a time which coincides with these dates.)

Hugo Beaumont 1717 (*Cambridge)

Luke Bedford 1722 (*Linton)

Judith Bennit 1654, Rob: Bennit 1674. (Although I was unable to find direct references to a family of this name in any of the parish registers which I searched, I did find a reference in the Linton registers which named a 'Mr. Bennit Justice of the Peace for the p'ish of Linton' during the seventeenth century.)

Richard Berry 1727 (?)

Charlotte Biggs 1787 (*Linton 1810)

Judith Bird 1620 (*Linton)

Rob: Bird 1756 (*Linton)

Soame Bird 1819 (*Linton)

Jacob Bishop (?)

Luke Bishop 1662 (?)

Joseph Blacke 1838 (?)

Richard Blacke his X mark 1770 (?)

Eleanor Blackwell 1757 (?)

Horace Blackwell 1791 (?)

Richard Blackwell 1740 (?)

John Bolton 1655 (*Linton 1823–43)

Alice Boorman 1507 (There is no record of a family of this name in any of the parish registers, which usually begin c. 1550 anyway; a family named BURMAN lived in Linton at the end of the sixteenth and the beginning of the seventeenth centuries.)

Jean Boormer 1737 (?)

Abraham Bowne 1726 (?)

Charles Bradley 1714 (There is no record in any of the Parish registers of a family of this name. However, there was at this time a large family living in Linton called BRADEY or BRADDY.)

Richard Bramwell 1842 (?)

Philip Brand 1662 (Born November 13th, 1629, of Philip and Hellen Brand,* Linton.)

Richard Brand 1720 (Baptised October 19th, 1688, of Philip and Ann Brand.)

Robert Brande 1655 (Baptised June 29th, 1631, of Robert and Anne Brand.)

Will: Brande 1662 (Baptised September 11th, 1640, of John and Margaret Brand.)

Alice Bray 1692 (Alice Trowell married William Bray, August 12th, 1632, in the parish of St Edward's, Cambridge. I do not know whether the name on the wall is that of this particular woman, or perhaps a daughter.)

Ferdinande Briande 1727 (?)

Amos Briggs 1747 (*Linton)

James Briggs 1757 (A James Briggs was baptised on April 15th, 1754. He married Elizabeth Pollard on June 12th, 1787. His parents were Robert Briggs and Abra Webb, who married in 1743.)

Francis Brilliarde 1696 (?)

Rebecca Brook 1810 (?)

Widow Brown 1662 (*Linton)

Ben Browne 1696 (*Linton)

Henry Browne 1672 (*Linton)

Humphrey de Browne 1455 (*Linton)

John Browne 1691 (A John Browne was baptised on January 18th, 1690. His father was also called John.)

Martha Browne (*Linton)

Ruth Browne 1710 (*Linton)

John Buck 1585 (*Linton)

Richard Bucke 1757 (This gentleman, described in the Linton Parish Registers as a carpenter of Debden, Essex, married Ann Skinner, July 28th, 1752.)

Thomas Buck 1632 (*Linton)

Thomas Bucke 1727 (John Buck, son of Thomas and Martha Buck, was buried, May 11th, 1756.)

Sarah Buckmeade 1808 (?)

John Burling 1655 (*Linton)

Lettice Burling 1647 (Baptised June 12th, 1608 of John and Mary Burling. Married William Webb, September 29th, 1641.)

Thomas Burling 1665 (*Linton)

John Burman 1727 (*pre-1634)

Susannah Burman 1737 (*pre-1634)

Thomas Burman 1722 (*pre-1634)

Thomas Burroughs 1660 (?)

Jane Butcher 1835 (?)

William Butcher 1702 (?)

Sarah de Buvais 1743 (?)

Daniel Byttin 1659 (Baptised January 22nd, 1648 of John and Anne Byttin.)

John Byttin 1701 (Baptised September 5th, 1632, of John and Anne. Died March 10th, 1703.)

Judith Byttin 1668 (Baptised December 21st, 1635, of John and Anne. Died January 15th, 1710.)

Ruth Byttin (*Linton)


C

Richard Camps 1710 (?)

Mary Canner 1888 (?)

Edward Carlen 1713 (Although I have been unable to trace this gentleman in any parish registers, I found a reference to him in the Electoral Rolls of 1705, 1722, and 1727. He stood as a candidate for the Whigs during the General Elections of those years. In 1705, Phillip, Richard, and Edward Webbe all voted for him; Philip and Edward again supported him during the Elections of 1722 and 1727.)

Thomas Carmbrooke 1667 (Baptised April 4th, 1630, of Peter and Anne Carmbrooke.)

Nicholas Carryer 1855 (?)

Henry Carter 1828 (*Linton and Horseheath)

James Carter 1819 (*Linton and Horseheath)

John Carter 1848 (*Linton and Horseheath)

John Casbolt 1818 (He married Mary Webb on September 5th, 1774 in Linton.)

Richard Casbolt 1702 (*Linton)

Charles Chalk 1707, Francis Chalk 1663, Jane Chalk, Jeremiah Chalk, Richard Chalke 1710 (Although there are records of this family in the Li .ton Parish Registers, the ˙ rliest record is after 1750. I would assume therefore that this family immigrated into the Linton area from another village, although I have not found reference to them in the parish registers of any other villages either. I do not believe that 'new' families suddenly appeared from nowhere as late as the mid-eighteenth century.)

Anne Chambers 1717 (She married Henry Webbe, June 18th, 1703.)

Nathaniel Chambers 1662 (*Linton)

James Chambers 1666 (*Linton)

Adame Chandler 1718 (?)

Elizabeth Chandler 1727 (?)

Henry Chandler 1717 (?)

Sam: Chaplin 1747 (?)

Richard Chapman 1702 (*Linton)

Sarah Chapman 1700 (*Linton)

Charles Churche 1686 (*Linton 1763–1838)

Henrietta Clarke 1656 (*Linton)

John Clarke 1733 (*Linton)

William Clarke ye Rector of Hadstocke 1715 (In his will of 1711, Robert Moore bequeathed 'one guinea to buy...a Ring to wear in remembrance of me' to William Clarke, Rector of Hadstocke in the county of Essex. Clarke was the Overseer of this will.)

Henry Clay 1740 (*Cambridge)

John Clements 1741 (He was buried in Linton on October 10th, 1756.)

Thomas Coas 1791 (I can find no reference to this gentleman in any of the parish registers in which I have searched. He obviously *did* exist as his signature is written on the fly-leaf of the book left in the house by Robert Webbe as an apport.)

Mary Cock 1734 (This lady was the second wife of Robert Webbe, senior. They were married on December 17th, 1710.)

James Cole 1799 (*Linton)

Robert Cole 1656 (He was baptised on June 8th, 1634, of Thomas and Marye Cole.)

Robert Cole 1710 (He was baptised on February 7th, 1650, the son of Robert Cole.)

Humphrey Coleman 1682 (*Linton 1714–66)

Eleanor Cooke 1710 (*Linton)

Penelope Cooke 1727 (*Linton)

Alice Cooper 1660 (*Linton)

Henry Cooper 1715 (*Linton)

Richard Cooper 1818 (*Linton)

John Costis 1668 (I have been unable to find records of a family by this name but there was a large family living in Linton called COTTIS.)

Sarah Cowle 1682 (*Linton)

William Cowle 1684 (Baptised June 8th, 1635, of William and Anne Cowle.)

John Cowling 1727 (?)

Henry Coxe 1733 (?)

Joan Coxe 1885 (?)

David Crane 1844 (*Linton)

John Crane 1733 (*This gentleman married Mary Webb, October 11th, 1732.)

John Crane 1828 (*Linton)

Sarah Crane 1737 (*Linton)

Walter Crane 1662 (This gentleman married Joan Veal, October 6th, 1685.)

Walter Crane 1727 (*Linton)

James Cricke 1733 (*Linton)

Oliver Cromwell 1643 (Born 1599, died 1658. Lord Protector of England, 1649–58. See 138–40)

Elizabeth Crutcheley 1756 (?)

William Crutcheley 1733 (Robert Webbe claimed that the front of the house was built by a William Crutcheley in 1731, although I can find no records of a family of this name in the area.)

William Crutcheley 1756 (?)

John Curtis 1757 (*Linton 1657–1713)

Henry Cutter 1739 (*Linton 1772–1840)

John Cutter 1797 (He married on April 8th, 1771, Anne Webb of Linton.)

D

Matthew Dalton 1677 (*Linton, 1563–1638)

Hugh Dandes, minister 1797 (This gentleman was minister of what was at this time the Linton Methodist Church. His gravestone records that he died in 1797.)

Edward Davies 1732 (This gentleman married Anne Webb, May 22nd, 1732, in Linton).

James Davies 1717 (*Linton).

Guy Deeling 1744 (?)

Alice Dockrile 1646 (*Linton)

Lawrence Dockrile 1654 (Baptised September 12th, 1583, and buried March 15th, 1656.)

Richard Duff 1757 (There is only one reference to the Duff family in the Linton Parish Registers. I found no other records of a family of this name in any other village. It would appear that this gentleman was a soldier, for in the records of baptisms in the parish of Linton is written, 'Ellin, daughter of Richd. of the Argile Fencibles, 18th. April, 1802'.)

Louis Dunnante 1707 (?)

Jean Dupont 1668 (?)

E

R.A.E. 1722 (?)

Edward Earle 1747 (*Cambridge and Linton)

Anne Embleton 1816 (Married Robert Webb, 14th. March, 1799.)

Anne Embleton 1838 (*Linton)

F

Charles Farmer 1827 (?)
Joseph Farrier 1799 (?)
Kathleen Farrier 1692 (?)
Betsy Field 1818 (?)
John Fielde 1727 (?)
Robert Fitche 1711 (*Linton)
Elizabeth Flack 1706 (Elizabeth, wife of John Flack of Linton, was buried July 1st, 1734.)
Robert Flack 1704 (Baptised July 2nd, 1662, son of Robert Flack, Gent., and Ann, his wife.)
Daniel Foxe 1619 (?)
Henry Foxe 1727 (?)
Daniel French 1749 (*Linton)
Daniel Fuller 1712, Dorothy Fuller 1717, James Fuller 1656, Richard Fuller 1757 (Although there was a family of this name living in Linton for a period during the eighteenth century, none of these members is recorded in the Linton Parish Registers. However, Fuller was a very common name in Cambridge and Gt Shelford at the same time.)

G

Richard Gates 1710 (*Linton 1812–40)
Henry Gardener 1810 (*Linton)
Stephen de Gardener 1545 (Although this gentleman is unrecorded in the parish registers of Cambridgeshire, I discovered that he had strong links with a family named Paris who lived in Linton. He was born about 1490 in Bury St Edmunds, about 25 miles from Cambridge. He went into the Church and soon became Cardinal Wolsey's secretary; he was employed by Henry VIII from 1527 to 1533, promoting in Rome and elsewhere his divorce from Catherine of Aragon. He was consecrated Bishop of Winchester in 1531. In 1537 he was posted to Paris where his secretary was Phillip Paris of Linton. In 1553 he was made Lord Chancellor of England by Queen Mary. He died in Whitehall of gout in 1555.)
Henri Gaucher 1727 (?)
Joanne Gaye 1718 (?)
Sarah Gaye 1756 (?)
Thomas Gayfer 1881 (There is an entry in the marriages section of the Linton Parish Registers, dated July 26th, 1825, which reads, 'Thomas Gayfer of Ashden in Essex married Martha Elizabeth Blackman'. His is the first name to appear on the deeds of Queen's House; he, 'and others', purchased the house for £520 in 1877 from John Kettle, taylor.)
John Glapcocke 1772, Joseph Glapcock 1878, Simon Glapcocke 1710 (There are no records at all of a family of this name having lived at any time in Linton or any other village in the area. However, there was a large family called GLAS-(s)COCK in Linton and I suspect that this spelling was an alternative version. As I have earlier explained, it was common for family names to be spelt in a variety of forms.)

Alexander Glascock 1657 (Baptised September 23rd, 1596. He married, at the Church of St. Mary the Less in Cambridge, Mary Webb, widow, on July 20th, 1632.)

R. Glascock 1735 (A Robert Glascock, son of Thomas and Elizabeth, was baptised October 31st, 1714.)

Benjamin Glover 1678 (?, but see below)

Margaret Glover 1679 (No family of this name existed at any time in the Linton area. I discovered the following entry, dated August 6th, 1636, in the parish registers of the Church of St. Edward's, Cambridge: 'Margarit Glover of Lolworth married Robert Kid of Swavesey.')

Anne Goodman 1749 (*Linton)

Issaac Goodman 1742 (*Linton)

Willheim van Graaf 1707 (?)

Anne Graile 1656 (?)

John Granger 1755 (*Linton)

Nathaniel Greene 1727 (*Linton)

Robert Griffith 1727 (?)

Nicholas Gunne 1818 (?)

H

C. H. 1777 (?)

Thomas Haddan 1833 (?)

Eleanor Halles 1505 (*Linton)

Phillip Halls 1787 (*Linton)

Richard Halls 1741 (*Linton)

Rob: Halls 1707 ('Mr. Robt. Hall of Lynton' was buried, September 5th, 1720, in Linton.)

Robert Halls 1674 (*Linton)

Nicholas Hammel 1828 (?)

Betsy Hammond 1833 (*Linton)

Charles Hammond 1699 (*Linton)

Luke Hammond (*Linton)

John Hammond 1622 (*Linton)

John Hammond 1669 (Baptised June 18th, 1656, of James and Elizabeth Hammond.)

John Hammond 1694 (Baptised November 18th, 1677, of John and Susannah Hammond.)

John Hammond 1828 (Baptised March 18th, 1811, of Joseph and Elizabeth Hammond. He married Rosette Webb, October 3rd, 1855.)

James Hampton 1718 (?)

Robert Handley (*Cambridge)

John Hardey 1733 (This gentleman married Mary Gastrell, November 10th, 1695, at St Edward's Church, Cambridge. In the registers of that parish, in which the marriage is recorded, both are described as being of Cambridge.)

Chas: Hardwicke 1820 (?)

Henry Hardwicke 1760 (?)

Eliz: Hart 1669 (*Cambridge)

Elizabeth Hart 1722 (In the parish registers of St Edward's, Cambridge, is the following reference to Elizabeth Hart in the baptisms section: 'June 16th., 1735, Sussanna, dau. of William and Elizabeth Hart'.)

P. Hart 1718 (*Cambridge)

Henry Hartley 1727 (?)

Richard Hartley 1757 (?)

Agnes Harvey 1505 (Although this date is approximately fifty

# Appendix 2

years before the year in which
Linton Parish Registers were
first kept, there is a reference in
the registers which reads,
'Agnes Harvey, widow, was
buried, 28th. April, 1591'. I
doubt if this is the same person
but I think it highly likely to
be the daughter, or perhaps
grand-daughter of the Agnes
Harvey whose signature is in-
scribed upon the wall; child-
ren were invariably named
after parents and relatives.)
Anne Harvey 1699 (An Anne
Harvey was baptised on
December 28th, 1700.)
Elizabeth Harvey 1811 (*Lin-
ton)
James Harvey 1700 (*Linton)
James Harvey 1757 (*Linton)
James Harvey 1891 (*Linton)
Sam: Harvey 1707 (Baptised
January 29th, 1689, of Samuel
and Mary Harvey.)
Simon Harvey 1658 (*Linton)
George Haris 1676 (*Linton)
Jonathan Harris 1700 (*Linton)
Daniel Harryson 1723 (*Linton)
Alice Haslop 1702 (*Cam-
bridge)
J. Haslop 1786 (*Cambridge)
Thomas Haslop 1786 (Thomas
Haslop of Thomas and Sarah
Haslop was baptised August
16th, 1747, at St Edward's
Church, Cambridge.)
John Hatcher 1855 (?)
Henry Hawkins 1742 (*Bartlow)
Susannah Hawkins 1780 (*Bart-
low)
John Hayes 1797 (?)
John Highcote 1827 (?)

Anne Highgate 1747 (?)
Dorothy Hill 1674 (*Linton)
Emma Hill 1801 (*Linton)
James Hill 1703 (*Linton)
Richard Hill 1820 (*Linton)
William Hill 1827 (*Linton)
Edward Hillman 1729 (?)
John Hinner 1712 (John Hinner,
(also spelt HINER, HYNER, and,
HINAH), lived in West Wrat-
ting with his wife named Eliza-
beth. In the parish registers of
this village are records of their
four children, Elizabeth, Mar-
garet, Sarah, and Mary. John
Hinner, described as a
labourer, was buried in West
Wratting in 1758.)
Katherine Hinner 1670 (*West
Wratting)
Sarah Hinnte (?) 1696 (?)
Hellon Hockley 1585 (Married
John Webb in 1564 according
to the Linton Parish Registers.)
Jane Hodson 1742 (*nineteenth
century)
Tho: Hodson 1707 (*nineteenth
century)
Robert Hogge 1726 (?)
Sarah Hogge 1785 (?)
Joane Hooper 1652 (*Linton)
Rebecca Horn (?)
Giles Horsemanne 1626 (?)
W. Horseman 1662 (?)
William Houldsworth 1592
(Vicar of Linton 1598–1602.)
Cecil Howarde 1555 (?)
James Howell 1812 (*Gt Shel-
ford)
John Howell 1717 (A John
Howell, son of Henry and
Alice Howell, was baptised,
October 27th, 1644, according

to the parish registers of Gt Shelford.)

Sophie Howell 1700 (*Gt Shelford)

James Hunter 1760 (*Linton)

Matthew Hunter 1699 (This gentleman was excommunicated in about 1685 with Robert Webbe according to the Linton Parish Registers.)

Henry Huppup 1692 (*Linton)

Elizabeth Hurst 1747 (*Linton)

Issaac Hurst 1686 ('Mr. Isack Hurst' was buried in Linton, May 17th, 1702.)

Issaac Hurst 1707 (Baptised September 26th, 1649, son of 'Isaack Hurst'. He married Anne Canham, April 27th, 1676.)

Philip Hurst 1707 (*Linton)

Amos Hutte 1798 (?)

Charles Hyman 1799 (?)

Charles Hymus 1855 (There is a reference to this gentleman, described as being of Horseheath, in the Linton Parish Registers in the baptisms section: 'James, son of Charles and Mary Hymus, 16th. February, 1843.')

Caroline Hynne 1828 (?)

## I

John Idleback 1505 (?)

Nath: Issaacson 1702 (*Cambridge and West Wratting)

## J

Charles Jackson 1844. (Married Elizabeth Nunn, November 11th, 1832, in Linton.)

Henry Jackson 1892 (*Linton)

James Jackson 1787 (*Linton)

Tho: Jackson 1723 (*Linton)

Amos Jeffries 1717 (?)

Alice Johnsone 1655 (*Linton)

Edward Johnson 1667 (*Linton)

John Johnson 1700 (*Linton)

Jone Johnson 1639 (*Linton)

Alice Jordan 1700 (*Linton)

John Jordan 1655 (Baptised June 24th, 1619, of John and Ellen Jordan, in Linton.)

## K

Daniel Keele 1728 (?)

Horace Keele 1717 (?)

Edmund Keene Rector 1777 (Vicar of Linton 1661–2)

John Kettle 1877 (This gentleman, described as a taylor in the deeds of Queen's House, sold the house in 1877 to Thomas Gayfer. Interestingly, his name, nor that of any member of his family, appeared in any of the parish registers.)

Edward Kidman 1660 (*Linton, post 1712)

Charles King 1747 (*Linton)

Eliz: King 1670 (*Linton)

James Kinge 1675 (*Linton)

Sam: Kinge 1772 (*Linton)

Katherine Knowles 1632 (Buried in Linton, June 12th, 1644.)

William Knowles 1696 (*Linton)

## L

Daniel Lacey 1833 (?)

Charlotte Lane 1739 (*Linton)

Thomas Langdone 1719 (?)

James Langmore 1757 (?)

John Legault 1555 (?)

Hugh LeNeve 1498 (Although this name is too early to trace easily, there was a family of this name living in a place called Witchingham who had connections with the Millicent family of Linton.)

Oliver Limpson 1690 (?)

Harriet Limstone 1709 (?)

Samuel Lindsay 1673 (Married Katherine Web, November 10th, 1670.)

Nathaniel Lister 1820 (*West Wratting)

Simon Littlechild 1700 (*West Wratting)

Harriet Livingstone 1828 (?)

Ebenezer Loade 1827 (?)

Israel Loade 1794 (?)

John Lockwoode 1797 (?)

Tho: London 1713 (*Linton)

George Long 1720 (*Gt. Wilbraham)

Daniel Longmere 1792 (I can find no record of a family with this name. There are references however to a family called LONGMIRE. Rev. Daniel Longmire was born in 1728, and died November 16th, 1789, according to the Linton Parish Registers. He and his wife, Elizabeth, had two children, Eulalia Maria, baptised 1780, and John Martyn, baptised 1781.)

Thomas Lonsdale 1767 (There is only one record in the Linton Parish Registers of a person with this surname. Christopher Lonsdale, M.A., Clerk, late of Stathern, Leics., died May 23rd, 1783. Since this family originated from Leicestershire, although having connections with Linton, could Thomas be a relative of Christopher?)

M

John Mabbutt 1856 (*Linton. Although the deeds for Queen's House go back only to 1877, I discovered from an enclosure map of 1842 that a family named Mabbutt occupied the house at the beginning of the nineteenth century.)

Betty Mailer 1902 (?)

Charles Manwaring 1727 (?)

John Marsden (?)

James Maul 1702 (*Linton, but usually spelt Mault)

Penelope Maul (Robert Webb, senior, married Penelope Mault, September 29th, 1685.)

John Maule MDCLXIII (1663) (Linton*)

John Maycock 1757 (?)

Richard McDonald 1856 (?)

Geoffrey Meade 1455 (*Linton)

Sam: Merton 1699 (?)

Harold Mervyn (?)

Chas: Miller 1700 (*Linton)

Robert Miller 1792 (*Linton)

Henry Millicent 1655 (*Linton)

Robert Millicent 1740 (*Linton)

Thomas de Millicent 1355 (Linton*)

James Moody 1767 (?)

Anne Moore 1662 (*Linton)

Robt. Moore 1692 (Buried May 20th, 1713.)

Robert Moore 1704 (Baptised September 24th, 1673 in Linton.)

Zillah Moore 1862 (*Linton)

Susannah Morcote 1703 (?)

Harriett Morecote 1755 (?)

John Morecote 1698 (?)

Robert Morecote 1800 (?)

James Moreson 1662 (?)

Anne Morley 1777 (*Linton)

Rich: Morley 1759 (*Linton)

Richard Morley 1797 (*Linton)

Sarah Morley 1848 (Baptised August 10th, 1799, of William and Mary Morley in Linton.)

Victoria Mortley 1858 (?)

Henry Mortlock 1820 (*Linton 1602–37)

Sarah Mortonne 1686 (?)

Tho: Mortonne 1703 (?)

John Mylon 1745 (?)

Robert Mylsent 1740 (*Linton.)

N

Joan Naylor (?)

Ellen Nicholls 1756 (*Linton, post 1823)

Charles Norton 1694 (*West Wratting)

Elizabeth Norton 1655 (*West Wratting)

Rachell Norton 1727 (*West Wratting)

Harriet Nunn 1858 (Married Charles Webb, 16th November, 1855, in Linton.)

John Nunn 1827 (*Linton)

O

Sarah Oakley 1721 (?)

William Oddle 1802 (There are no records of a family of this name, although a family who spelt their name ODELL, lived in Linton.)

Amos Onyon 1702 (*Linton)

John Onyon 1677 (John Onyon of Linton was buried January 18th, 1701.)

John Onyon 1702 (John Onyon of Linton was buried September 13th, 1719.)

Robert Ottway 1717 (*Linton, but OTWAY)

Agnes Oubonet 1589 (?)

Johanne Oubonnet 1626 (?)

P

Hugh Page 1787 (*Linton)

Jane Page 1667 (*Linton)

Walter Page 1667 (*Linton)

William Page 1679 (Baptised April 29th, 1638, of William and Elizabeth Page.)

Phillip Paris, Knight 1558 (Born 1492 and died 1558. He was a member of the prominent Paris family of Linton and was knighted by Queen Mary at her coronation. He took a prominent part in the suppression of the monastries and attended the King and Queen at the Cloth of Gold. He worked with Stephen Gardener, whose signature also appears on the wall, as a secretary, and went with him on his embassy to Paris in 1537.)

Thos: de Parise 1365 (*Linton)

Henrietta Parker 1677 (*Linton)

Matthew Parker 1677 (*Linton)

Rich: Parker 1727 (*Linton)

Agnes Parrye 1605 (*Linton)

Courtenay Partridge 1747 (* Linton, pre-1695)

Elizabeth Partridge 1720 (*Linton, pre-1695)

Robert Partridge 1646 (Baptised December 26th, 1596, son of Richard Partridge.)

John Patten 1686 (There are no records in the Linton Parish Registers of a family of this name at this date. However, a John Patten married Susannah Webb, September 19th, 1782.)

Barnabas Paye 1683/4 (There is a record in the Linton Parish Registers of the marriage of Anne Webbe and Barnabas PAGE in 1662.)

Edward Paye 1771 (?)

Luke Pearce 1910 (?)

Charles Peting 1693 (?)

Randolph Pick 1718 (?)

Richard Pinter 1760 (?)

John Pitcher 1720, John Pitcher 1797, Robert Pitcher 1662 (I have found no record of a family of this name in Cambridgeshire but there was a large family in the Linton area called PITCHES.)

Katherine Pitches 1677 (The only reference in the Linton Parish Registers that I could find relating to this person was in the baptisms section. It read: 'Robert son of Robert and Katherine Pitches, 19th. February, 1643'.)

Jeremiah Place 1777 (?)

Gregory Pope 1777 (?)

Oliver Porter 1690 (?)

James Potter of Hildersham 1710 (*Hildersham)

James Price 1717 (?)

Tho: Punter 1666 (Vicar of Linton 1649–60 and 1663–85.)

R

Henry Randall 1713 (*Linton, late eighteenth century.)

James Randall 1707 (*Linton, late eighteenth century.)

Mary Randall 1705 (*Linton, late eighteenth century.)

Amos Rawlinson 1717 (*Linton)

Elizabeth Rawlinson 1840 (John Rawlinson married Elizabeth Pammenter, May 12th, 1801, in Linton.)

Benjamin Reynolds 1656 (*Linton)

Henry Richardson 1770 (*Linton)

William Richardson 1820 (Married Mary Ellen Webb, August 8th, 1854, in Linton.)

Jane Richmond 1778 (*Linton)

Luke Richmonde 1717 (*Linton)

Stephen de Richmonde 1500 (*Linton)

Thomas Richmonde, sen. 1700 (Baptised February 19th, 1631, of Barnabie and Anne.)

Enoch Roach 1797 (?)

John Robertson 1772 (Baptised in Gt Abington, January 7th, 1724, of Richard and Bridget.)

George Robinson 1756 (*Linton)

Issaac Robinson 1827 (*Linton)

Richard Robinson 1838 (*Linton)

William Robinson 1719 (*Linton)

P. Rogers 1759 (*Linton)

Elizabeth Rucke 1651 (There are references in the parish

registers of St Edward's, Cambridge, to a family of this name of Ospringe, Kent.)

Charles Rule 1655 (*Linton)

Margaret Rule 1657 (Married John Webb, farmer, 1663.)

Barbara Rutland 1674 (?)

Simon Rutland 1674 (?)

Simon Rutland 1705 (?)

Edward Ryder 1779 (*Linton)


S

Philip Sadler 1773 (?)

Thomas Salmone 1620 (*Linton. On a map of Linton, dated 1620, Thomas Salmon is shown as being the occupant of Queen's House.)

Isaac Samson MDCLXII (1662) (?)

Mary Sanderson 1866 (*Weston Colville)

John Sawbridge 1838 (?)

Henry Seaman 1705 (*Linton)

Alice Seeley 1654 (I found only one reference to a family of this name in any of the parish registers in which I looked. It was a record in the Carlton registers of the burial of Thomas Seeley in 1629.)

Elizabeth Shore 1667 (?)

Hannah Shore 1707 (?)

Lucy Simons (*Linton)

Anne Simpson 1700 (*Linton)

Samuel Smallbody 1620 (?)

Samuel Smedley 1808 (?)

Daniel Smith 1793 (*Linton)

Elizabeth Smith 1802 (*Linton)

William Arnold Smith 1860 (*Linton)

Isiah Smoothy 1699 (*Linton)

Richard Smoothey 1777 (*Linton)

Joshua Sparrow 1719 (*West Wratting, Weston Colville, Carlton)

Margaret Sparrow 1720 (A Margaret Sparrow married Thomas Penny of Denny Abby at St Edward's Church, Cambridge, April 3rd, 1665.)

Barbara Speede 1733 (*Linton, post 1835)

Charles Speede 1690 (*Linton, post 1835)

Anne Stinton 1727 (Anne wife of William Stinton of Weston Colville was buried December 9th, 1729.)

James Stinton 1692 (*Linton, Weston Colville, West Wratting, and Gt Wilbraham)

James Stinton 1757 (*Linton, Weston Colville, West Wratting, and Gt Wilbraham)

Margaret Stinton 1701 (*Linton, Weston Colville, West Wratting, and Gt Wilbraham)

Martin Stinton 1858 (*Linton, Weston Colville, West Wratting, and Gt Wilbraham)

Rebecca Stinton 1658 (*Linton, Weston Colville, West Wratting, and Gt Wilbraham)

Rebecca Stinton 1718 (*Linton, Weston Colville, West Wratting, and Gt Wilbraham)

William Stinton 1696 (There were five men with this name living in Linton at this time.)

Sam: Stopps 1673 (?)

Robert Stubbin 1696 (*Linton)

Thomas Stubbin 1677 (*Linton)

John Summerton 1763 (*Linton)
Richard Swanne 1723 (*Linton)
Eliz: Sykes 1656 (?)
Jane Symonds 1646 (*Linton)
John Symonds 1702 (*Linton)

**T**

Katherine Le Taillour 1555 (*Linton, TAYLOR)
Thomas the tailloure 1495 (*Linton, TAYLOR)
Daniel Tanner 1688 (*Carlton)
Oliver Tanner 1898 (*Carlton)
Dan Tauter (?)
G. B. Tayler 1815 (*Linton)
Arthur Taylor 1827 (*Linton)
Elizabeth Taylor 1863 (*Linton)
John Taylor 1818 (*Linton)
Robert Taylor 1677 (*Linton)
William Taylor 1688 (*Linton)
Eleanore Tench 1710 (*Cambridge)
Jeremiah Tench 1655 (*Cambridge)
Daniel Thompson 1775 (*Linton)
Rich: Thorne 1758 (*Gt Shelford)
Rich: Thurling 1797 (?)
T. Tippings 1685 (Vicar of Weston Colville at this time was Thomas Tippings.)
Issaac Tobin 1666 (?)
Thomas Tofts 1633 (*Linton)
George Trench 1717 (?)
Francis Trowbridge 1698 (?)
George Turner 1828 (*Linton)
John Turner 1732 (*Linton)
Mary Turner 1753 (*Linton)
Ed: Tylher 1655 (*Linton, a form of TAYLOR)

**U**

Widow Unnyer 1684 (*Linton, a form of ONYON)

**W**
**T.W.**
John Waile 1888 (?)
Charles Waitte 1708 (*Linton)
Margaret Wakefield 1792 (*Linton)
Rich: Wakeling 1750 (*Linton)
Joshua Waterly 1696 (?)
Henry Watkins 1877 (?)
Henry Watts 1828 (*Gt Shelford)
John Web 1552 (Married Hellon Hockley in 1564.) Frederic Webb 1855 (*Linton)
John Webb 1746 (Married Ann Page, 1725. Died August 14th, 1746.)
Martha Webb 1747 (Died July 23rd, 1752.)
Noah Webb 1833 (*Linton)
R. S. Webb 1818 (*Linton)
Richard Webb 1766 (Richard and Sarah, twins of Richard and Elizabeth Webb, were baptised November 6th, 1756.)
Anne Webbe 1736 (Married Robert Webbe, junior, April 6th, 1714.)
Hannah Webbe 1652 (Second wife of Richard Webbe, father of Robert Webbe, senior.)
Henry Webbe my house 1678 (Father of Millicent Webbe, and husband of Ruth.)
James Webbe 1727 (Son of Robert Webbe, senior. Baptised September 26th, 1703. Buried November 15th, 1737.)

Capt. James Webbe 1739 (*Linton)

John Webbe junior 1715 (Son of Robert Webbe, junior. Baptised August 5th, 1716)

Richard Webbe 1703 (Husband of Hannah Webbe; father of Robert Webbe, senior.)

Richard Webbe 1756 (Richard and Sarah, twins of Richard and Elizabeth Webb, were baptised November 6th, 1756.)

Rob: Webbe (I believe this to be the signature of Robert Webbe, senior.)

Rob: Webbe 1733 ( This is the signature of Robert Webbe, junior.)

Sarah Webbe 1697 (Married John Webbe and died in 1750.)

John Wells 1767 (*Linton)

Rich: Wells 1755 (*Linton)

Robert Wells 1755 (*Linton)

Albert West (*Linton)

J. West 1721 (*Linton)

Rebecca West (*Linton)

Robert West 1712 (*Linton)

Penelope Westmoreland 1700 (?)

Elizabeth Wheeler 1837 (* Linton)

Sarah Whiffin 1806 (*Linton)

Richard Whiteheade 1690 (?)

Ruth Willaos (?) 1667 (?)

James Willcocks 1830 (?)

Eleanor Williams (*Linton)

Luke Wills 1717 (*Linton, but WILLIS)

Joan Wilton 1655 (*Gt Shelford)

Nicholas Winter 1801 (*Linton)

Godfrey Woodhouse 1585 (?)

Henry Wooler 1744 (?)

Giles Wright 1642 (*Linton)

Y

James Yates 1763 (*Cambridge)

Inscribed upon the walls are 544 names which can be divided into 296 different family names. Of these 296 family names, I have managed to find 182 of them in the parish registers in which I have looked. I have no idea of the significance of the date: it is not a date of birth, and rarely a year of decease. Obviously the date is of relevance to the person whose name appears on the wall, but it remains, to me, a mystery.